INSCRIBED WITH LOVE AND REVERENCE
TO THE MEMORY OF
MY FATHER AND MOTHER

PREFACE

THIS manuscript was begun early in the fall of 1921 as a study in the diplomatic relations existing between the United States and Great Britain during the Spanish-American War. It was soon discovered that official negotiations of the two countries could only be understood when they were considered in connection with the record of contemporary public opinion. Consequently the plan was altered and enlarged for the purpose of coördinating the study of governmental documents with a critical review of the periodical literature and other source material that might serve to show the interplay between governmental action and public opinion.

The writer wishes to acknowledge grateful appreciation for the many courtesies extended her during the preparation of the study. Sincere thanks are due to Professor B. F. Shambaugh for the privileges granted in the library of the State Historical Society of Iowa and to the officials and attendants of the Chicago Public Library, Newberry Library at Chicago, the Company Library at Philadelphia and the Library of Congress at Washington. In the latter institution Dr. Charles Moore of the Manuscript Division rendered valuable assistance in securing a number of very helpful interviews and much unpublished material.

She is grateful to Professor H. G. Plum of the State

University of Iowa whose kindly suggestions have been a source of much encouragement. Especially is she indebted to Professor A. M. Schlesinger, also of the State University of Iowa, whose critical comments and careful advice have been of inestimable value both in the search for material and in the preparation of the manuscript.

CONTENTS

ANGLO-AMERICAN RELATIONS
DURING THE
SPANISH-AMERICAN WAR

Anglo-American Relations During the Spanish-American War

CHAPTER I

ANGLO-AMERICAN BACKGROUND

A prejudice or opinion when cherished by a people through several generations becomes embedded in common belief. The latter stage having once been reached, the feeling or judgment of the people is no longer susceptible to calm reason or sane argument. Such was the force of the anti-British feeling held by a great many Americans at the beginning of the last decade of the nineteenth century. It was an hostility rooted in colonial history and handed down by successive generations, each one finding some new grievance to add.[1]

An analysis of those factors which tended to hold the

[1] A number of general discussions of the attitude of the American people toward Great Britain are of particular interest: Adams, George Burton, *Why Americans Dislike England* (Philadelphia, 1896); Wister, Owen, *A Straight Deal or the Ancient Grudge* (New York, 1920); Dos Passos, John R., *The Anglo-Saxon Century* (New York and London, 1903); Gardiner, A. G., *The Anglo-American Future* (New York, 1921); Hale, S. Reynolds, *A Little Tour in America* (London, 1895).

United States and Great Britain apart is essential in order to appreciate the force of their friendship engendered in the nineties and brought to fruition by the Spanish-American war.

The beginning of this anti-British antipathy is found in the inherent character of the early colonial settlers who, to a very marked degree, were composed of people too radical either in religion or politics or both to live peaceably in their original home. This characteristic of temperament, added to the facts that the colonists possessed almost exclusive control both in their local government and religion and that they were three thousand miles distant from the homeland, created an intense feeling of colonial authority and self-sufficiency. The result was the development of a new theory of colonial rights and privileges which led the colonists eventually into the Revolution. Great Britain thus became recognized by the Americans not as the most lenient and beneficent colonizing nation of the seventeenth and eighteenth centuries, but as a tyrant and an oppressor of subject states. This interpretation, due to the force of tradition and faulty methods of instruction, has tended to continue among the mass of the American people ever since.

With the establishment of peace in 1783 the Americans found that their relations to their former mother country had changed in a significant, and not altogether favourable way. The same war which had brought them independence had also deprived them of the special rights and privileges of trade which they had enjoyed as members of the British empire. Besides this, the British still held the western forts; rumours that Great Britain was about to turn loose upon the West the horrors of Indian warfare persisted; and Jay's treaty, negotiated somewhat later in an effort to solve these difficulties, aroused an outburst of indignation. Finally, the British misuse of the right of search, together with the commercial difficulties incident to the Napoleonic wars, led the United States into a second war with England.

An unpopular and indecisive war followed. After peace was restored the Americans rapidly developed an air of buoyancy and self-confidence which was often interpreted as youthful insolence. At heart, however, many of them were anxious for British praise and acceptance of all that they did. As a result all adverse criticism was repeated and remembered while all comments of praise were accepted as a matter of course and forgot. Unfortunately, as time passed, British writers hurled upon the Americans criticism after criticism which contained just enough of unpleasant truth to make them exceedingly exasperating and unfair. Many, if not most, of the Americans were described as being lawless, ignorant, crude, and rude. Their newspapers were pronounced unreadable and their press reporters overzealous while travel was slow and full of discomfort. Their social activities were poorish, their travelling manners were abominable—they talked loudly, spat frequently and vigorously, and behaved ostentatiously. Actually, America was a frontier country with its usual mixture of good and bad, desirable and undesirable, refinement and crudity. A traveller saw whatever he might look for, and a few British stirred up an American antagonism which one hundred years of peace have since failed to eliminate entirely.[2]

During Jefferson's presidency the United States began a policy of active continental expansion in which Great Britain held an interest scarcely secondary to that of the United States. British supremacy in Europe was dependent, in part, upon the restrictions of continental colonial and commercial expansion in the New World. The revolt of the Spanish colonies in South America combined with the threatened interference of the monarchial powers of Europe in behalf of Spain aroused the apprehension of both the United States and Great Britain. Consequently, in 1823, George Canning, British minister for foreign affairs, suggested to Richard Rush, the American minister to Great Britain, the expediency of an understanding between the United States and Great Britain on the question of the Spanish colonies. Such a policy of joint action was inconsistent with the isolated position previously maintained by the United States and with her own national welfare. As a result the United States acted upon her own initiative and proclaimed the Monroe Doctrine which did not limit British trade expansion but which did restrict European colonial expansion.

From such a background of Anglo-American discords a series of situations developed which constantly added fuel to Anglo-American hostility for over fifty years.

---

[2] Dickens, Charles, *American Notes* (London, 1843); Trollope, Frances, *Domestic Manners of the Americans* (London, 1828); Seybert, Adam, *Statistical Annals of the United States* (Philadelphia, 1818).

In the first place, the Monroe Doctrine unmistakably made the two states rivals rather than joint actors in the struggle for control of affairs in the Western Hemisphere.[3] In the next place, because of this rivalry, conflicts of interest incident to the development of Canada, to the promotion of trade, and to relations with the British West Indies, constantly occurred.

With the outbreak of the Civil War, the states of the Union found several reasons for additional hostility toward Great Britain. Some members of the British upper classes, together with the cotton manufacturers, expressed open sympathy for the South. This friendship was due to a number of causes. To begin with, British industry was involved. Great Britain required a constant and regular supply of cotton. Much of this was purchased from the South and any war would be sure to interrupt cotton shipments. Besides this, the South preferred free trade. Furthermore, the South had always been more closely related to the British in temperament, in religion, in education, and in ideals than had the North.[4] Immediately upon the outbreak of the war a few Englishmen began to compare the causes of the Civil War as they were enunciated by the South with the causes of the Revolution as they had been advanced by the colonists. The colonists had asserted that government was just only when sanctioned by those governed. Since the South did not sanction the federal government then

---

[3] Dunning, William Archibald, *The British Empire and the United States* (New York, 1914), p. 55.

[4] *Cf.* Pierce, Edward Lille, *Memoirs and Letters of Charles Sumner* (Boston, 1877-1893), Vol. VI, p. 159.

certainly it had as much right as did the thirteen
colonies to set up an independent state. If this were
true, then Lincoln was obviously a second George III.[5]

In May, 1861, the Queen issued a proclamation of
neutrality. To the North, which considered the war
purely a domestic question and looked upon the Con-
federacy as an organization of rioters and traitors,
the British proclamation seemed hasty, if not hostile.[6]
In November of the same year another grievance arose
when Captain Charles Wilkes stopped the *Trent,* a
British mail steamer, and seized Messrs. James Mur-
ray Mason and John Slidell, Confederate commissioners, as prisoners. Immediately British opposition
assumed a serious aspect and Lord Palmerston, the
British premier, and Lord John Russell, secretary for
foreign affairs, demanded the release of the men.[7]

Scarcely was the *Trent* affair closed when another
difficulty arose between the two countries. In 1862,
the *Florida,* a Confederate cruiser built in Liverpool,
sailed for the Bahamas. Later in the same year, in
spite of the efforts of Charles Francis Adams, the
American minister at London, the *Alabama,* a second
destroyer, sailed from the same port for the Azores.
By 1863, due to the more stringent neutrality of the
Palmerston government and to the persistent efforts
of Mr. Adams, three other destroyers, then being constructed under the same conditions as the *Alabama*
and the *Florida,* were prevented from leaving Liver-

[5] Dunning, *op. cit.,* pp. 200-203.

[6] Moore, John Bassett, *A Digest of International Law* (Washington, 1906), Vol. VI, p. 6.

[7] *Ibid.,* Vol. VII, pp. 768-779.

pool.   Aggressive agitation over these violations of neutrality continued until 1871 when Great Britain accepted the Geneva award.

Unfortunately, a number of factors served to minimize the propitiation of this compromise in the eyes of both the Americans and the British.   Canada was seething with unrest, and revolt seemed possible.   The United States recognized this and felt that Great Britain's acquiescence in the Geneva decision was due to fear of American intervention in Canada.   Furthermore, J. C. Bancroft Davis, who represented the United States in the Geneva Conference, had demanded remuneration not only for direct losses but for indirect losses, due to the exclusion of American shipping from the seas and for the general expense of maintaining the war after July, 1863.   His failure to secure these sweeping demands only served to arouse further American hostility against Great Britain.

Another source of American prejudice was to be found in the anti-British agitation stirred up by Irish immigrants and Irish-American citizens.   Mr. Alexander Mackay who visited the United States as early as 1846 said: "In the Irish population of the United States is the true source of the enmity towards this country which is sometimes exhibited.   Originating among these, unscrupulous politicians fan the flame to serve their own purposes. . . ." [8]   In 1865, Great Britain began to combat actively the Fenian agitations in Ireland; and with the suspension of the Habeas Corpus Act of 1866, large numbers of Irish

[8] Mackay, Alexander, *The Western World* (Philadelphia, 1849), Vol. II, p. 294.

fled to the United States. Gradually a Fenian army numbering in all about twelve hundred was recruited from among the Irish immigrants and restless demobilized Irish-American Civil War veterans for the purpose of invading Canada. The invasion was checked by prompt action on the part of the American government but not before actual depredations had been committed or the agitation had stirred up much bad feeling both in the United States and Great Britain.

After 1867, Irish agitators in America devoted their energies persistently toward the prosecution of the Irish cause. New York, Boston, Philadelphia, Chicago, and St. Louis fell under their domination and became centres of propaganda. Their offices were filled with Irish incumbents and their taxes became the prey of Irish graft. A number of other cities of lesser importance fell equally under their influence. So far as state elections were concerned, it is impossible to determine the extent of Irish influence. It is safe to say, however, that in a number of cases senators and congressmen, angling for Irish-American votes, were elected who used their offices very largely as a means of promoting Irish politics. Irish influence in national elections is even more difficult to estimate. But again it seems safe to say that while they may not have been directly responsible for controlling a considerable number of votes, Irish enthusiasm for political expression undoubtedly gave them an influence out of proportion with their actual number.[9] Besides this, tens of

[9] Consult the following party platforms for references to the Irish question: Democrat, 1868, 1876, 1884, 1888, 1892; Republican, 1868, 1872, 1876, 1884, 1892.

thousands of dollars were raised throughout the United States, both for the support of suffering Irish in Ireland and for the prosecution of Irish propaganda and home rule.[10]

Another important though somewhat intangible cause of Anglo-American antagonism was to be found in certain common racial characteristics. As members of the same family are prone to criticize each other most sharply, so were the British and Americans, once members of the same empire. American sensitiveness on the one hand felt and resented English criticism keenly. English travelers in the United States, accustomed to English ways and conveniences, resented their absence in the United States and refused to adapt themselves to the strange surroundings. On their return home they forgot to be charitable in their descriptions. The gentle old English lady of long

[10] O'Brien, R. B., *Life of Charles Stewart Parnell, 1846-1891* (New York, 1898), *passim; Congression Record*, 48th Congress, 2d session, Vol. XVI, pp. 983, 997, 1000, 1007, 3755, 4073; *ibid.*, 51st Congress, 1st session, Vol. XXI, p. 10397; *Foreign Relations*, 1884, p. 216; *ibid.*, 1885, p. 445; *ibid.*, 1887, pp. 520-521, 539-540; Merwin, Henry Charles, "The Irish in American Life," *Atlantic Monthly*, Vol. LXXVII (March, 1896), pp. 289-301; Russell, T. W., "American Side-Lights on Home Rule," *Fortnightly Review*, Vol. LIX (March, 1893), pp. 340-351; Lowell, A. Lawrence, "Irish Agitation in America," *Forum*, Vol. IV (December, 1887), pp. 397-407; Matthews, Byron C., "A Study in Nativities," *ibid.*, Vol. XXVI (January, 1899), pp. 621-628; O'Shea, John J., "Irish Leaven in American Progress," *ibid.*, Vol. XXVII (May, 1899), pp. 285-296; Bocock, John Paul, "The Irish Conquest of Our Cities," *Forum*, Vol. XVII (April, 1894), pp. 186-195; "The Extradition of Dynamite Criminals," *North American Review*, Vol. CXLI (July, 1885), pp. 47-60; "The Irish in America," *Westminster Review*, Vol. CXXIX (June, 1888), pp. 713-732; *New York Nation*, March 20, 1884, January 29, 1885.

generations of aristocratic training resented keenly the kind but crude courtesy which prompted the railway conductor to call her "Grandma" as he gave her the most gracious assistance possible.

As better traveling facilities developed and wealth increased, large numbers of Americans flocked to England. Many of them were socially untrained people who had recently acquired financial independence and were in no way representative of American culture. British magazines and newspapers ridiculed these people in cartoon and description. British critics constantly revealed the superiority which they felt; they denied a common civilization, yet resented whatever in America differed from that in Great Britain. Thus a common language had its objection for it enabled the people of the two countries to learn all the petty comments made by the other. All this anti-British criticism found its way into the American educational system. Particularly was this true in the study of history where writers have too often seen fit both to interpret unfairly from the American point of view and to magnify all American accomplishments in order to instill lessons of national pride and patriotism. "Writers of school histories have thought it necessary to provide strong food for little minds. Entirely out of focus are the trifling details that the colonists were English; that they had the freest self-government then known to mankind; that at least a third of the people in the colonies were opposed to independence; that no taxes were ever laid on the colonies for the support of the government or military authorities outside of America; and that a strong minority in England were opposed to the war [Revolution]." [11]

Strong as was the centrifugal force that had been operating for over a century /between Great Britain and the United States, it was opposed and gradually counteracted by a centripetal force ever more powerful. In the first place most of the colonists were Anglo-Saxons. To them Great Britain was home. Their self-imposed exile only intensified their feeling of kinship. Just as the individual, deprived of his own home through his own actions, often appreciates for the first time the real significance of that home, so the colonists, frequently critical and hostile toward Great Britain, often maintained within their inner consciousness a profound feeling of kinship.

Sharing the same language, the English literature with its wealth of tradition and history became also the possession of the colonists. It was, indeed, the primal and fundamental bond existing between them. *The King James Bible,* Cranmer's *Book of Common Prayer,* Foxe's *Lives of the Martyrs,* and the old English hymns, together with Milton's *Paradise Lost* and Bunyan's *Pilgrim's Progress* were the treasured and essential volumes in every American library. In fact, it was not until nearly a quarter of the nineteenth century had passed that there can be said that an American literature existed.

[11] Hart, Albert Bushnell, Preface to *Documents* 39-49, Association for International Conciliation, American Branch (Washington, 1897); *Cf.* Hart, A. B., *School Books and International Prejudices,* American Association for International Conciliation (New York, 1911); Altschul, Charles, *The American Revolution in Our Textbooks* (New York, 1917).

During the colonial period and the early part of the nineteenth century, cultured Americans, particularly those of the South, went to England for a portion of their education. The training received during their years abroad, combined with a common racial inheritance and literature, led to a community of thought which served to unite the people of the two countries in a fixed friendship. It is true that it was a one-sided relationship in the beginning, for Great Britain received American ideas with reluctance, but as time passed a common philosophy, ethics, and political theory served not only to reveal mutual interests and sympathies but an actual unity of fundamental principles and ideals. For example: the Puritan Sunday of Cromwell became the Puritan Sunday of Increase and Cotton Mather; the faith of the Wesleys and George Whitefield became the faith of the Methodists in America; the attitude of the Baptists toward the state in England became the attitude of the Baptists toward the state in Rhode Island. British common law became the basis of American common law; Sir William Blackstone became the foremost authority for American jurists; Jeremy Bentham and the English Utilitarians became the exponents of American social legislation; while the great British reform bills of the nineteenth century contained little that had not found previous expression in the United States.

A common legal and constitutional theory has probably been one of the leading factors in promoting Anglo-American friendship. Edmund Burke, in a speech delivered before the House of Commons in 1775, asserted that nearly as many copies of Blackstone's *Commentaries* had been sold in the colonies as in England. For over a hundred years it was considered the foundation of all legal education in America. A British magazine put it thus: that the courts of Michigan are more Anglo-Saxon than those of Edinburgh.[12] Specific differences there were but the underlying principles and ideals were usually identical.

In the determination of the status of the Irish-American, common legal theories have always been utilized to maintain peace. In 1866, the Fenians planned to send an expedition composed of Irish-Americans, Civil War veterans and Irish immigrants from New York against Canada. A proclamation of neutrality was immediately issued by the President warning all citizens against the violation of the laws of neutrality and exhorting the United States officials to employ all their lawful authority to defeat the expedition and to bring to justice all persons engaged therein.[13] This declaration was in entire harmony with the previous American demand, fully complied with by Great Britain, that Canada should not in any way be used by the Confederates as a base of their military operations. Again in 1866 naturalized Irish-Americans when arrested while traveling or sojourning in Ireland upon complaints of complicity in seditious proceedings began to demand protection accorded by their American citizenship. Mr. Charles Francis

[12] "Are the Americans Anglo-Saxons?" *Spectator,* July 30, 1898.

[13] *Public Laws of the United States,* 39th Congress, 1st session, Appendix p. iii. This proclamation was embodied in the form of a House Bill and passed in the House with a large majority. *Cf. Congressional Globe,* 39th Congress, 1st session (July 26, 1866), p. 4193.

Adams, minister to Great Britain, read to the Earl of
Clarendon a confidential dispatch from William Henry
Seward, secretary of state, which has served as a solution of that question ever since. Mr. Seward declared
that Americans "whether native born or naturalized
owe submission to the same laws in Great Britain as
British subjects while residing there and enjoying the
protection of the British government. . . ." [14]

For a period of nearly fifty years American theories
of democracy had served as a source of irritation between the two countries but in 1830 the Whigs, under
the leadership of Earl Grey, as prime minister, came
into power with a policy of internal reform. With the
adoption of the Reform bill of 1832 Great Britain entered upon an era of democratic development that was
to continue throughout the century.[15] One event after
another occurred to shorten the distance between the
two political systems.[16] During the Civil War when

[14] Flower, B. O., "Federation of the Anglo-Saxon Races," *Arena*,
Vol. XX (August, 1898), pp. 223-238; *Cf.* Gladden, Washington,
"Are the Americans Anglo-Saxons?" *Spectator,* July 30, 1898.

[15] In 1835 De Tocqueville's [Alexis Charles Henri Clérel] volume,
De La Democratie En Amérique, was published. The same year
the author visited England, where the Whigs gave him a most
enthusiastic welcome. During that visit De Tocqueville, who was
a student of American democratic principles, gave them their first
unbiased and scholarly interpretation in England.   Fortunately
Richard Cobden's pamphlet *England, Ireland and America* appeared
contemporaneously with the former great study. As a member of
the Manchester school American democratic principles not only
found considerable favour with him but he announced for the
first time that Great Britain's chief interest lay in the promotion
of her economic welfare through the development of Anglo-American
trade.

[16] Dunning, *The British Empire and the United States,* pp. 68-87.

William E. Gladstone and Lord Palmerston spoke for the upper middle classes and the titled aristocracy, and John Bright and Richard Cobden spoke for the lower middle and working classes, the friendship of the latter with the North and the former with the South represented alliances between people of common political ideals in both cases.

The victory of the federal government in the United States and the Liberals in Great Britain represented a common victory for democracy. "As a matter of fact, a fundamental influence in fixing the sympathies of the Britons was the more or less unconscious perception of a relation between the American problem and their own. The liberalizing and democratizing spirit was disintegrating both the old political parties. Those who welcomed this spirit longed for the preservation intact of the American union as the model of a great and prosperous democracy. Those who dreaded the approach of democracy were quick to see in the American war a proof of its weakness and futility." [17]

With the great English middle class in control of British politics, as it was after the great reform bills of 1867 and 1885 were passed, the two countries drew rapidly together as a result of their common democratic ideals. Speaking of this latter-day British regard for American democracy, Mr. James Bryce said, "Rather than being dreaded as a fountain of democratic propaganda, America is looked upon as the champion of

[17] *Ibid.*, pp. 228-229; *Cf.* Schurz, Carl, "The Anglo-American Friendship," *Atlantic Monthly,* Vol. LXXXII (October, 1898), pp. 433-440.

popular government against the great military monar-
chies of continental Europe." [18]

Other characteristics much more intangible than
those thus far mentioned but which contributed greatly
to draw the British and Americans together include
common moral and social ideals, and a profound respect for the family and the home based largely on
the influence of the mother. These led to free inter-
marriage with little or no question of social differences.
Thus it was that, in spite of frequent and bitter differences, a number of fundamental forces were operating
to bring the two countries together. Common theories
of law, government, and social order were being rapidly
revealed. Great Britain was accepting American
theories of democracy. The United States, having successfully passed through the formative period of democratic political organization, was accepting British
theories of ordered administrative development. New
ties of kinship, mutual regard, and national interest
were displacing old ideas of suspicion and selfish
competition.

[18] Bryce, James, "The Essential Unity of Britain and America,"
Atlantic Monthly, Vol. LXXXII (July, 1898), pp. 22-29.

CHAPTER II

THE INTERNATIONAL BACKGROUND

BY 1890 it was apparent to thoughtful students of world politics that the next decade would bring a complete readjustment of international relations. One cycle of events was drawing to a close; another, having already assumed definite form, was ready to emerge into a tangible and concrete existence. The new imperialism which had been developing since the Franco-Prussian War had assumed important aspects and proportions. Old international alliances were outgrown and new ones were in process of formation.

In 1887, the Triple Alliance, composed of Germany, Austria, and Italy, had been renewed. Three years later the Russo-German Convention and the Three Emperors' League was abandoned. The significance of these two events was fourfold. It marked a victory of the north German merchants over the conservative national policy of Bismarck. It freed Germany from the possibility of being dragged into the Russo-British quarrels in Europe and Asia. It left her in position to make the most of the situation should she be dragged into the Russo-Austrian quarrels in the Balkans. It left the Triple Alliance as the only active European alliance while the other three great states, Great Britain, France, and Russia, stood isolated.

17

Gradually Russia discovered that her natural hostility toward Germany made closer relations with France advisable. This induced her to borrow vast sums of money from France for the promotion of internal improvement and industry. At the same time Russia kept a constructive foreign policy in mind. She would block German expansion on the west, British expansion in the Near East, and both German and British expansion in China. In France the dominating policy was anti-Germanic. France had neither forgot nor forgiven the Franco-Prussian peace settlement, but so long as Bismarck had been in power his pro-Russian policy had prevented the consummation of an alliance between France and Russia which their common interests required. In 1891, the French fleet landed at Cronstadt. The *Marseillaise* was played at the Tsar's request while he stood at respectful attention. In 1893, the Tsar returned the visit by calling at Toulon. The two rulers exchanged complimentary telegrams and the Tsar made allusion to the bonds that united the two countries. Thus was laid the basis of a Franco-Russian alliance, the protocol of which was actually signed in 1891. The military agreement followed in 1894.

So far as Italy was concerned, the Triple Alliance had been signed for protection only. She feared both the French policy of expansion in Africa and the Austro-Hungarian occupation of Trieste and Trent. Furthermore, in the Adriatic region, there were still a number of Italian communities not yet incorporated into the Italian state which were being closely watched by the dual monarchy. Finally, Italy feared European intervention in behalf of the papacy. In 1882, the friendly overtures of Bismarck, together with the French imperial policy, had driven Italy into the German alliance. Just how strong this alliance was when it was renewed in 1887 it is difficult to say. Soon after 1890, however, it began to be evident that Italy was not wholly comfortable in her European alliance. She had begun to transfer her fear from France to Austria, her natural enemy in the Adriatic, and her confidence from Germany to Great Britain.

Great Britain, in the meantime, stood as she had been since the Crimean War, alone in her "splendid isolation." In 1895, the Conservative party, led by the Marquis of Salisbury and supported by Joseph Chamberlain, came into power with a new policy of colonial expansion and imperial solidarity. This policy, if adopted, would serve to destroy the existing balance of power as well as Great Britain's scheme of isolation. A program of aggressive colonial expansion would bring her immediately into direct conflict with the dominating member of each of the European alliances. Great Britain would thus be forced to prepare to meet the possibility of a combined alliance of the two groups of powers or else to forsake the policy of expansion as advocated by the Salisbury administration. The latter neither political party was willing to do for, strange to say, while the Conservative party had initiated the new policy, the Liberal party was fully committed to it; and, backed by a strong newspaper sentiment, and a powerful minority in the House of Commons, censured severely what they considered the dilatory or feeble policy of the Conservatives.

Thus the Liberal leaders of the Opposition were in full harmony with the foreign policy of the Conservatives, but, due to their failure to understand the danger of Great Britain's isolation, they urged prompt and decisive action.

On the other hand, the Conservatives, due to the diplomatic foresight and influence of Mr. Joseph Chamberlain and Lord Salisbury, appreciated the danger which Great Britain, without allies, or without assured colonial support, was facing in territorial and commercial expansion in Africa and in the East; and they were doing their utmost to block any possible union between the two military alliances of the continent. Especially helpful for their purpose were the intense Franco-German hatred and the friendship of Théophile Delcassé of the French colonial office, 1893-1898, for Great Britain. But for all immediate or practical purposes Great Britain stood isolated, facing the possibility of an attack by each of the two alliances. Should she have been forced into such a war under existing conditions, she would have, in all probability, been seriously defeated. It was this perilous isolation which the Salisbury ministry faced and understood and which the Opposition failed to appreciate—an isolation whose significance was stated openly and frankly on May 13, 1898, by Joseph Chamberlain in an address to his constituency at Birmingham.

This address set forth three fundamental propositions: first, that Great Britain had maintained a policy of strict isolation since the Crimean War, but now a new situation had arisen and she was liable to be confronted at any moment with a combination of the Great Powers; second, that it was her first duty to draw all parts of her empire closer together and to infuse into them a spirit of united and imperial patriotism; third, that it was her next duty to establish and maintain bonds of permanent amity with her kinsmen across the Atlantic.[1] If this scheme could have been executed and a definite alliance been formed between the British Empire and the United States it would have given to the English speaking countries the balance of world power, and, at the same time, it might have nullified the two European alliances and restricted the German and Russian policies of colonial and commercial expansion.

While the two great European alliances were assuming definite organization, a new power appeared in international politics. By 1890 the United States, a western nation hitherto unrecognized as a force in world politics, had come to be openly involved in the Far East. This situation which had been developing for a century had come about so gradually and so naturally that the majority of the people of the nation were generally unaware of either its growth or its existence. It had come as the normal result of the expansion of its industry and commerce. There were four different spheres around which this trade had developed: the Hawaiian Islands which were in the path of trade between the United States and China; Japan which was both an objective in itself and in direct line with China; and Samoa which was in the path of trade both between the United States and Australia, and

[1] *London Times,* May 14, 1898.

Panama and Australia. The fourth sphere included a group of guano islands scattered far and wide throughout the Pacific.

As early as 1800, Honolulu had become a base for fur traders operating between the Pacific Northwest, China, and the New England states. By 1820 American missionaries had entered the Hawaiian islands, and in September of the same year John C. Jones was appointed to reside there as the agent of the United States for commerce and seamen. As early as 1842, Daniel Webster pointed out the commercial significance of Hawaii to the United States when he said that since most of the vessels which visit the islands belong to the United States, she was therefore more interested in their fate and government than any other nation could be. This consideration led the president to declare that the integrity and sovereignty of their government should be maintained.[2] From this time on the question of Hawaiian annexation remained before the American people. In January, 1893, a revolution broke out in Honolulu. The abdication of the Queen was secured and a provisional government was set up which continued until annexation with the United States was complete. On February 15, President Harrison submitted such a treaty to the Senate. Two sentences of the accompanying message indicated the attitude of the administration toward expansion. "It is essential that none of the other great powers shall secure these islands. Such a possession would not consist with our safety and with the peace of the world." [3]

[2] Moore, *International Law Digest*, Vol. I, pp. 476, 482.
[3] *Ibid.*, p. 497.

With the return of the Democratic party to power the treaty of annexation was withdrawn from the Senate by President Cleveland. In the next few years American commercial interests in the Orient developed rapidly. This, together with the outbreak of the Spanish-American War, indicated the imperative necessity of annexation which was finally effected in July, 1898.

Japan, the second centre of American activities, was developed largely through the influence of a few traders and statesmen who saw the necessity for prompt action if American prestige was to be maintained in the East. In 1832, Edmund Roberts was sent by President Jackson to investigate commercial possibilities in the Indian Ocean. He was instructed to obtain information respecting Japan, the means of beginning communication with it, and the value of its trade with the Dutch and Chinese. In 1846, Commodore James Biddle was sent to open Japan to American trade and failed. A second expedition sent out five years later under Commodore Matthew C. Perry was successful. The Townsend Harris treaty of commerce and navigation, drawn up soon after this, 1858, in an effort to forestall European action, indicated the future attitude of the United States toward trade in the Far East.[4]

As early as 1853, if not earlier, the United States was represented by a commercial agent at Apia in the Samoan islands. The following year a consul was provided. In 1872, Commander Richard W. Meade entered into an agreement with Chief Maunga of the Bay of Pagopago in the island of Tutuila which pro-

[4] *Compilation of Treaties in Force* (Washington, 1899), pp. 327-332.

vided for the establishment in that harbour of a naval station for the use and convenience of the vessels of the United States. About this time traders began to urge the growing importance of the Samoan trade with the result that in 1873 the United States government sent a special agent there for investigation. From then on trouble between the nations interested in Samoan trade, Great Britain, Germany, and the United States, grew in proportion to the determination of each to increase her trade. After 1884 German statesmen undertook a systematic policy of expansion in the islands. The United States and Great Britain, previously in control of the Samoan trade, objected strenuously. By the close of the decade, American popular interest had reached such a pitch that American warships were sent to defend her trade. With American, British, and German warships gathered there, each nation determined upon the protection of commercial interests, trouble seemed inevitable. Fortunately, a hurricane swept the island at an opportune moment. The good feeling engendered as a result of the sincere coöperation extended in the work of rescue led to the compromise of 1889 in which the three nations agreed to a policy of joint control. The real significance of the episode lay in its prophetic nature. Germany had contended vigorously for foreign monopoly of the trade of the islands. The United States had contended with equal force for open trade under native control, protected, if need be, by American guarantee. This policy of joint control existed until 1900 when the islands were divided between the United States and Germany.

By 1856 the guano industry in the Pacific had become of sufficient importance to warrant legislative administration and control. It was accordingly enacted that territory yielding guano, discovered by citizens of the United States and not in the possession of subjects of any other country, might, at the discretion of the President, be considered as belonging to the United States. Further legislation guaranteed rights of inheritance, established the price of guano, extended the laws of high seas over the islands, and finally authorized their protection by the use of naval and land forces. During the decade of the eighties the United States had appropriated and extended temporary control over no less than fifty guano islands.[5]

By about 1890, therefore, there had developed in the Pacific a new maritime area of international commercial activity destined to be the scene of an intense struggle for trade and colonial expansion in the coming era. This field was to hold in the closing years of the nineteenth century the same significance as had the North Atlantic a little more than a century earlier.

Six nations were to operate in this field: France which was pledged to avenge her defeat of the Franco-Prussian War; Italy which aspired to the rank of one of the great nations in Europe; Russia which had entered upon a new program of expansion in northern Asia and the Near East; Germany which had just inaugurated a new policy of commercial expansion and colonial conquest in the Near East, Asia, Africa

[5] Moore, *op. cit.*, pp. 565-580.

and Oceanica; Great Britain whose naval supremacy had remained unchallenged for a century and which sought to dominate the new expansion in the Orient and the Pacific as she had the earlier expansion in the North Atlantic; and, finally, the United States. They represented the two great alliances of Europe with Great Britain and the United States as isolated powers, the very danger of whose isolation was bound, sooner or later, to bring them into contact with each other.

Two new policies were destined to influence commercial expansion in the new area. The United States was responsible for both of them. Upon her entrance into Oceanica she had carried with her the same theories of trade that she held in the Western Hemisphere. These provided briefly that all undeveloped areas should be subject to native control and that the native governments should grant equal trading opportunities to all foreign nations. In order to secure this condition the United States had negotiated treaties with Hawaii, Japan, and Samoa. President Tyler, in his message of December 30, 1842, spoke concerning Hawaii. Any attempt, he said, by any power to take possession of the islands, colonize them, and subvert the native government could not but create dissatisfaction on the part of the United States. The United States seeks no peculiar advantages, no exclusive control over the Hawaiian government. Its forbearance in this respect would justify the American government, "should events hereafter require it, in making a decided remonstrance against the adoption of an opposite policy by any other power." The following year, 1843, Great Britain renounced a deed of cession of the Hawaiian islands on the demand of the United States, declaring the act entirely unauthorized by Her Majesty's Government. A few years later these principles were incorporated in the treaty of 1849.[6] The treaty of 1858, with Japan, was equally specific. After outlining the two principles which the United States maintained should govern the development of new areas, the treaty continued, "The president of the United States, at the request of the Japanese Government, will act as friendly Mediator, in such matters of difference, as may arise between the Government of Japan and any European Power." [7] The treaty of friendship and commerce of 1878 with Samoa was similar in nature. "If, unhappily, any differences should have arisen, or shall hereafter arise, between the Samoan Government and any other government in amity with the United States, the government of the latter will employ its good offices for the purpose of adjusting those differences upon a satisfactory and solid foundation." [8] Great Britain acquiesced in the American policy in the Pacific as she had in the Western Hemisphere. This acquiescence laid the basis, as will be seen later, for future Anglo-American relations in the Far East.

Three causes were operating to promote intense rivalry among the European nations who were expanding in this new sphere of commercial activity. They

[6] Cf. Treaty of December 20, 1849, *ibid.*, p. 479; and *ibid.*, *passim*, pp. 476-482.

[7] Cf. Treaty of July 29, 1858, *Compilation of Treaties in Force* (1898), pp. 327-331.

[8] Cf. Treaty of January 17, 1878, *ibid.*, pp. 551-552.

were the same as those which had induced them to enter upon a new policy of colonial aggression. New fields of trade would give increased power. They would likewise serve as a source of supply for raw material, but above all, they would afford a market for manufactured goods and a field for the investment of capital.

The causes of American expansion were much the same. By 1890, the frontier of the United States had disappeared and national consciousness had begun to find expression in international politics and commercial enterprises. Capitalists who had formerly found a field of investment in undeveloped home territories, and manufacturers whose products had been consumed in the home market now sought a foreign market. The annexation of colonial territories and the opening of new avenues of commercial activity were the logical result.

The indirect causes which had led to this expansion were likewise common. Rapid means of communication had shortened distances. Missionary zeal had opened up vast areas hitherto little known. Scientific progress had created scores of new wants and new commodities to supply those wants. Methods of agriculture had been improved, manufacturing and industries of all sorts were producing a surplus of goods. In fact, with the exception of the United States, all of the countries involved had probably outgrown the bounds of their original territory, both in capital and population. Either territorial expansion or national stagnation seemed inevitable to them. The natural result of this progress was an unprecedented increase in the volume of industry and commerce, with a corresponding growth in national rivalry.

The international situation of the last decade of the nineteenth century, therefore, can be understood only in the light of the various conflicting movements of national expansion which found expression in Asia, Africa, and Oceanica. In the gradual development of affairs three factors of peculiar interest to Great Britain and the United States had assumed significance; that by 1890 the United States was committed to a policy of aggressive commercial expansion; that that policy must inevitably lead her into European international politics; and that the beginning of an Anglo-American trading policy in opposition to the current European methods of expansion had already been laid in Samoa and Hawaii.

In 1890, Captain Alfred Thayer Mahan began an active effort to draw the attention of the two great English speaking races to this intimate association which was slowly developing between them. In that year he published his first great naval study, *The Influence of Sea Power upon History, 1660-1783.* A second study was published in 1892, *The Influence of Sea Power upon the French Revolution and Empire.* These were followed by a number of short articles in prominent American magazines.[9] Through them all

[9] Mahan, A. T., "The United States Looking Outward," *Atlantic Monthly,* Vol. LXVI (December, 1890), pp. 816-824; *ibid.,* "The Isthmus and Sea Power," *Atlantic Monthly,* Vol. LXXII (October, 1893), pp. 459-472; *ibid.,* "Hawaii and Our Future Sea Power," *Forum,* Vol. XV (March, 1893), pp. 1-11; *ibid.,* "Possibilities of an Anglo-American Reunion," *North American Review,* Vol. CLIX (November, 1894), pp. 551-573; *ibid.,* "The Future in Relation to

the author sought to convey two central ideas to the general public: that the destiny of nations is explicable only through a study of the potency of sea power and that British sea power was closely related to American progress. The extent of the influence exerted by Captain Mahan was probably very great. Thousands of people, both British and American, began to realize, for the first time, the close relation that was developing between the two countries.[10] It was this relation which was destined to have a large part in the direction and control of international politics during the next decade.

American Naval Power," *Harper's New Monthly Magazine*, Vol. XCI (October, 1895), pp. 767-775. These articles together with a number of others were published in volume form later with the title *The Interest of America in Sea Power, Present and Future* (Boston, 1898).

[10] *Cf.* Taylor, C. Carlisle, *Life of Admiral Mahan* (New York, 1920), pp. 42-52, 61-77, 112-118.

CHAPTER III

The Period of Transition, 1890-1897

Although over eighty years of uninterrupted peace had passed since the treaty of Ghent was signed, relations between the United States and Great Britain had never become friendly. Open hostility and sincere friendship each found expression as occasion warranted. It seemed as if only an event so important that it threatened the welfare of both nations would be able to remove the hostile sentiments existing between the two nations and promote a feeling of friendly relationship. Such an event actually occurred in 1895 when the Venezuelan boundary controversy was suddenly added to the perplexing problems which Great Britain was already facing in European politics.

In June, 1895, the Marquis of Salisbury, coalition leader of the Conservatives and the Liberal Unionists, came into power. At the general election held one month later his appointment was confirmed by the return to parliament of a majority of one hundred fifty-two of his adherents. This unequivocal victory was largely due to the adoption of a new foreign policy, for Great Britain was determined to restore her former international prestige. As has already been suggested, the Salisbury program involved the formation of an international alliance of such strength as would assure Great Britain the balance of world power. The natural sources for such a combination were to be found in the loyalty of the British colonies and in the United States.

The new Government included a group of men of varied interests and unusual political ability. Mr. Arthur Balfour became first lord of the treasury and leader of the House of Commons. Sir Michael Hicks Beach was chancellor of the exchequer; Mr. Joseph Chamberlain, colonial secretary; and Lord Salisbury, prime minister. So far as the United States was concerned the last two appointments were by far the most significant. In general, those people of the United States who know Lord Salisbury both feared and hated him. They thought him reactionary, conservative, autocratic, and aristocratic. At the same time, they considered him not only the greatest man of his own party, but by far the most influential British citizen of the time. Furthermore, as a firm believer in an aggressive foreign policy, it was inevitable that he should influence Anglo-American relations in the Pacific.

Mr. Chamberlain, a Liberal Unionist in politics, was the most energetic, the most dynamic, and probably the most popular member of the cabinet. Coming as he did from Birmingham, a manufacturing centre, and considered the friend of all British manufacturing interests, he spoke for British trade the world over.[1] As early as 1888 he had stated publicly that the future of Great Britain was inseparably bound up with that

---

[1] Low, Sidney, and Sanders, L. C., *History of England During the Reign of Queen Victoria* (William Hunt and R. L. Poole, ed., *The Political History of England*. Vol. XII), (London, 1907), p. 431.

of her colonies and the United States. With the former, he advocated a commercial union and a union for defence; with the latter, a "durable friendship." [2] The opportunity to carry out his policy came with the election of Lord Salisbury and the adoption of the new British foreign policy. Mr. Chamberlain was given what had previously been considered a relatively unimportant portfolio. His plan, however, was to make the office of colonial secretary the pivotal position in the promotion of the new British foreign program. Within six months after his appointment Mr. Chamberlain was actively engaged in the prosecution of his plans.[3]

The new Coalition Government was plunged immediately into foreign complications. The revival of Armenian persecutions by the Turks brought the Near Eastern question into prominence. It was here that Lord Salisbury received American criticism for the first time, since many Americans placed upon the British full responsibility for the continuation of the Armenian atrocities. The situation was even more serious in the Far East. Chitral was permanently garrisoned, an event which meant the revival of Anglo-Russian competition in Indian territory. The Chino-Japanese War showed China to be a decadent nation; and Russia, France, and Germany, each prepared for immediate

[2] Speech before the Devonshire Club, April 9, 1888, *Mr. Chamberlain's Speeches,* Charles W. Boyd, ed. (London, 1914), Vol. I, 318-324.

[3] On August 22, 1895, Mr. Chamberlain presented his first statement of his colonial policy in Parliament. *Cf. The Parliamentary Debates* (Hansard's), Fourth series, Vol. XXXVI (August 22, 1895), pp. 639-643.

aggression, began at once to seek concessions and "spheres of influence." In Africa the British faced a variety of problems, for the entire continent was being opened to foreign conquest. General Charles Gordon's death in the Sudan had not yet been avenged. French interests were being asserted throughout the North. German expansion was moving forward so rapidly toward the South that it threatened not only to prevent further British expansion, but to jeopardize the British colonies already established there.

Since Lord Salisbury proposed to prosecute an active foreign policy, it was necessary that he should meet all of these situations at once. But Great Britain was without allies; and every one of the nations which he would oppose was a member of one of the two great European alliances. Thus, Lord Salisbury was limited to a policy of diplomacy, for war could be justified only upon the greatest provocation. Into this crisis in British affairs an event of unusual significance was now projected.

On December 29, 1895, Dr. Leander Jameson made his famous raid into the Transvaal. This was followed on January 3, 1896, by a friendly note from the German foreign office to President Paul Kruger.[4] A few days of frenzied activity on the part of the British Government followed, and the "Flying Squadron" was made ready for action. War seemed almost inevitable. Immediately promises of sympathy and support arrived from the principal British colonies. It had been understood for some time that Mr. Cham-

---

[4] Eckardstein, Baron von, *Ten Years at the Court of St. James,* 1895-1905 (London, 1921), pp. 82-86.

berlain had been engaged in investigating conditions in the colonies, and this event served as an opportunity for him to announce both British dependence on colonial loyalty and his policy of imperial federation.

On January 21, 1896, a dinner was given in honour of Lord Lamington, who was leaving England to assume his duties as governor of the colony of Queensland.   After having spoken of the greatness of the Australian colonies, Mr. Chamberlain called attention to the South African affair and to the significance of the assurances of colonial support in case of war. Then, quoting from Tennyson, he said, "let

> 'Britain's myriad voices call,
> "Sons, be welded each and all,
> Into one Imperial whole,
> One with Britain, heart and soul!
> One life, one flag, one fleet, one Throne!" ' " [5]

Serious as the Anglo-German episode may have been it was exceedingly opportune in that it served to crystallize the policies of the new British Government and to reveal to the British people the fundamental weakness of their international position.   This weakness having once been demonstrated, it became possible for Mr. Chamberlain to urge the second step in his foreign policy—the promotion of a "durable friendship" with the United States.   His opportunity came when the Venezuelan boundary controversy was projected into the complication of British affairs in December, 1895.

[5] Speech at Whitehall Rooms, London, January 21, 1896, Chamberlain, *op. cit.,* Vol. I, pp. 359-365.

The boundary line between the Republic of Venezuela and British Guiana had never been accurately determined. About 1840 settlers began to enter the disputed region and the two Powers concerned became determined to secure possession of as much territory as possible. The controversy which resulted was not an important one. There were no great theories of international law nor any delicate international agreements previously arranged to be disturbed, whatever might be the result of the boundary controversy. Considered from this latter standpoint, the Anglo-German affair in South Africa, or the protection of the Armenians was of far greater significance. A number of events, however, had recently occurred which stimulated both American and Venezuelan interest in the disputed area. European trade rivals, particularly Great Britain and Germany, had begun to encourage their trade in Venezuela.[6] This fact led a few American merchants and consuls to investigate means of furthering American trade. In December, 1886, the United States, for the first time, officially offered arbitration in the boundary controversy if acceptable to both countries concerned.[7] By 1891 the United States had definitely begun to abandon her attitude of disinterestedness and to urge upon Great Britain the need of arbitration. American concern in the boundary controversy seemed to develop in proportion to the efforts of American traders to encourage

[6] *Consular Reports,* Vol. XLIV (February, 1894), p. 389; *ibid.,* Vol. LIV (April, 1897), p. 474; *Commercial Relations of the United States with Foreign Countries,* 1894-1895, Vol. I, pp. 527, 532.

[7] *Foreign Relations of the United States,* 1895 (Washington, 1896), part 1, pp. 549-550.

American interest in Venezuela.[8]   In his reports for December, 1894,[9] and July, 1895,[10] Mr. E. H. Plumacher, the American consul at Maracaibo, earnestly advocated American intervention as a means of securing trade advantages.   Besides this, the discovery of gold and the realization that the Orinoco River controlled the trade of about one-fourth of the continent encouraged a few Venezuelans to urge upon the American merchants and the American department of state the necessity of intervention.[11]

Throughout the year 1895 sentiment developed rapidly in the United States in favour of intervention. In his second annual message of December 3, 1894, President Cleveland suggested that he would renew the efforts heretofore made to bring about a restoration of diplomatic relations between Great Britain and Venezuela and to induce a reference of the question to arbitration.[12]   On February 20, 1895, Congress passed a joint resolution recommending the favourable consideration of the President's suggestion.[13]   The reasons for American intervention, as brought out dur-

[8] *Consular Reports*, Vol. XXVIII (December, 1888), pp. 20-22; Vol. XXIX (April, 1899), pp. 758-762; Vol. XXXIII (August, 1890), p. 03; Vol. XXXIX (May, 1892), pp. 184-185; *Commercial Relations of the United States with Foreign Countries* (Washington, 1894), 1892-1893, pp. 341-393; 1894-1895, Vol. I, pp. 525-530; 1895-1896, Vol. , pp. 148-149.

[9] *Ibid.*, Vol. I, pp. 527-529.

[10] *Consular Reports*, Vol. IXL (October, 1895), pp. 204-207.

[11] *Congressional Record*, 53d Congress, 3d session, Vol. XXVII, part , p. 1833; *Foreign Relations*, 1895, part 1, p. 559; *Consular Reports*, Vol. L (April, 1896), pp. 446-447.

[12] Richardson, James D., *A Compilation of the Messages and Papers of the Presidents* (Washington, 1898), Vol. IX, p. 526.

[13] *United States Statutes at Large*, Vol. XXVIII, p. 971.

ing the debate in the House of Representatives, were three in number: the maintenance of the Monroe Doctrine; the protection of Venezuela in her demands for the possession of the mouth of the Orinoco River as essential to her commercial development; and the promotion of American trade interests in Venezuela.[14] In July, Mr. Richard Olney wrote his famous Venezuelan note to Great Britain. The controversy, he said, was one in which both American interests and honour are involved and the continuance of which it cannot regard with indifference. While it was one of the most undiplomatic notes ever drawn up by an American secretary of state, it succeeded in calling out an immediate statement of the British attitude toward the new interpretation of the Monroe Doctrine as it had been presented by President Cleveland. The note left but two possibilities open for the settlement of the boundary dispute—war or arbitration.

Great Britain's position was precarious and her national honour was involved. War with the United States was an impossibility, both because of the immediate delicacy of the British international position and because it must of necessity preclude any Anglo-American "durable friendship" for a period of years. On the other hand, any obvious display of hasty conciliation was liable to be interpreted, both in the United States and in Europe, as an evidence of internal weakness.

On November 26, 1895, Lord Salisbury sent a reply

[14] *Congressional Record,* 53d Congress, 3d session, Vol. XXVII, part 2 (February 6, 1895), p. 1833, part 3 (February 16, 1895), p. 2297.

o the Olney note. It was an example of British
diplomacy at its highest degree of efficiency. Realiz-
ing that his reply would eventually be made public,
he outlined his dispatches in such a manner that while
they met British popular demands they served both as
an answer to Mr. Olney's note and as information for
the Americans. The Monroe Doctrine, he said, while
sound in theory, was not a part of international law
and could not be interpreted as covering the determination of the frontier of a British possession. He concluded with a complete statement of the British case
in Venezuela, the first that had been given.[15] On
December 17, President Cleveland sent a special message to Congress in answer to Lord Salisbury which
was hardly more tactful than Secretary Olney's note.
He asserted that American intervention in the boundary controversy was within the original scope of the
Monroe Doctrine, that the Monroe Doctrine was recognized in international law, and that Great Britain had
refused arbitration. In conclusion he asked Congress
to authorize a special commission to investigate and
ascertain the true divisional line between Venezuela
and British Guiana. "When such a report is made and
accepted it will in my opinion be the duty of the United
States to resist by every means in its power as a
willful aggression upon its rights and interests the

[15] *Foreign Relations,* 1895, part 1, pp. 563-576. A few months later
a reprint of Senate Document No. 226 was called for because there
was but one copy of it available for the use of Congress. This document was a statement of the boundary controversy from its beginning
down to July, 1888. For a copy of it see *Senate Executive Documents,* 50th Congress, 1st session, Vol. XI, 1887-1888 (Washington,
1888).

appropriation by Great Britain of any lands or the exercise of governmental jurisdiction over any territory which after investigation we have determined of right belongs to Venezuela. In making these recommendations I am fully alive to the responsibility incurred, and keenly realize all the consequences that may follow."[16]

Whatever may have been President Cleveland's motive in presenting such a warlike message, it had two far-reaching results. It served as a definitive statement of his new interpretation of the Monroe Doctrine and the danger of its threat served to call forth an expression of Anglo-American opinion both in the United States and in Great Britain. It became, however, a peace message, forcing the expression of mutual good will to such an extent that it overcame the ill will which was likewise expressed.[17]

On the same date, December 17, the Olney note and Lord Salisbury's reply were given to the American public.[18] People were amazed. Many knew that trouble had been brewing but only a few realized that the Government was actually creating a crisis that under ordinary circumstances would produce war. Immediately every anti-British element in the country was turned loose. Out of this confusion there grad-

---

[16] *Foreign Relations,* 1895, part 1, pp. 542-545.

[17] *Cf. British Annual Register,* 1895, part 1, new series, p. 378. This is one of the best accounts of the reception given the message by Congress, Wall Street, the public and the "jingoes"; Gladden, Washington, *England and America* (London, 1898), pp. 23-26; *Public Opinion,* December 26, 1895.

[18] *Congressional Record,* 54th Congress, 1st session, Vol. XXVIII part 1, pp. 191-198.

ually came the voice of deliberation. A few pleas for
justice, for delay and for British friendship were made
in Congress.[19] Then came a fall in stocks and bonds.[20]
On December 19, a memorial was read in the Senate,
signed by three hundred fifty-four members of the
British House of Commons, advocating a treaty of
general arbitration.[21] On December 20, Congress voted
to place $100,000 at the disposal of the President to
provide for the expense of a commission which should
investigate and report upon the true divisional line
between the Republic of Venezuela and British
Guiana.[22] Then came the Christmas season with its
spirit of good will. Passion was tempered by sentiment. From thousands of pulpits and scores of re-
ligious publications all over the land came indignant
denunciations of the war craze. Equally insistent was
the almost unanimous expression of the colleges and
universities.[23] Influential people of both countries at
once recognized that diplomats had produced the crisis.
They demanded that the same diplomats should find
a way to save the honour of both nations by means
of peaceful negotiations.[24]

In Great Britain the President's message generally

[19] *Ibid.*, pp. 240, 242, 244, 246, 247, 258, 260, 261.
[20] *Ibid.*, p. 261.
[21] *Ibid.*, p. 24.
[22] *Statutes at Large*, Vol. XXIX, p. 1.
[23] Gladden, *England and America*, pp. 26-30; *New York Nation*,
January 2, 1896; *Literary Digest*, January 4, 1896; *Public Opinion*,
January 2, 1896.
[24] For the development of American opinion consult *New York
Nation*, December 19, 26, 1895, January 2, 9, 1896; *Literary Digest*,
December 21, 28, 1895, January 4, 1896; *Public Opinion*, December 19,
26, 1895, January 2, 9, 1896.

brought surprise and horror. On December 24, an
appeal was issued by British authors, signed with
thirteen hundred names, urging their confrères in
America to use every possible means to avert a fratri-
cidal war.[25] During the same week a series of British
peace messages, originally sent to the *New York World,*
appeared in various papers throughout the United
States. Among the contributors were the Prince of
Wales and Duke of York, Cardinal Vaughn, Archbishop of London, Archbishop Walsh of Dublin, and
Mr. Henry Labouchère. Just after President Cleveland's message went to Congress, William Watson
made the great British poetic appeal:

"O towering Daughter, Titan of the West,
  Behind a thousand leagues of foam secure;
  Thou to whom our inmost heart is pure
  Of ill intent: although thou threatenest
  With most unfilial hand thy mother's breast,
  Not for one breathing space may earth endure
  The thought of War's intolerable cure
  For such vague pains as vex to-day thy rest!
  But if thou hast more strength than thou canst spend
  In tasks of Peace, and find'st her yoke too tame,
  Help us to smite the cruel, to befriend
  The succorless, and put the false to shame
  So shall the ages laud thee, and thy name
  Be lovely among nations to the end." [26]

Suddenly Great Britain's attention was directed
to the South African situation. On January 2, 1896,

[25] *Public Opinion,* January 2, 1896.

[26] Watson, William, "England to America" in *The Purple East*
(London, 1896), pp. 25-26, an early copy may be found in *Public
Opinion,* January 9, 1896.

the Jameson raid met with its humiliating defeat, and
on the following day the congratulatory note from the
German Emperor to the Boer President was made
public. Besides this, Great Britain was threatened
with trouble in the Far East and in Turkey.

On January 1, 1896, President Cleveland announced
the appointment of the boundary commission. The
task before the commission proved of unexpected difficulty. Early in February, Mr. Thomas Bayard,
American ambassador to Great Britain, asked Lord
Salisbury that the British facilities be placed at their
disposal.[27] Strange as the request was, it was so
promptly and graciously granted that the reply served
to attract quite a little attention in the United States.[28]
Early in February, Parliament went into session. It
immediately recognized the seriousness of the situation
and adopted a spirit of conciliation. The Queen spoke
first in behalf of peace.[29] Immediately the Opposition, led by Sir William Harcourt,[30] and the Government, led by Sir Arthur Balfour,[31] began to vie with
each other in offers of conciliation. Both accepted
the Monroe Doctrine; both admitted the right of
American intervention in Venezuela; both announced
their friendliness toward the American boundary commission, and both asserted their willingness to arbi-
trate. The climax in the discussion came when Lord

[27] *Foreign Relations*, 1895, part 1, p. 576; *ibid.*, 1896, pp. 243-247;
British State Papers, Vol. LXXXVIII (1895-1896), p. 1242.

[28] *Ibid.*, p. 1243; *Foreign Relations, op. cit.*, p. 576.

[29] *Parliamentary Debates* (Hansard's), Fourth series, Vol. XXXVII
(February 11, 1896), pp. 3-6.

[30] *Op cit.*, February 11, 1896, pp. 81-105, 511-515.

[31] *Ibid.*, pp. 105-118.

Salisbury himself concurred in all that Mr. Balfour said.[32]

It was inevitable that arbitration should grow out of the American assurances of good will and the British offers of conciliation. On February 27, 1896, the American Government proposed to Lord Salisbury that negotiations be begun at once at Washington in an effort to settle the boundary controversy. The British Government agreed and on November 12, 1896, a treaty of arbitration was signed. The treaty for settlement was finally signed on February 2, 1897.[33] But the fundamental result of the Venezuelan boundary controversy was not the establishment of the frontier line of an undeveloped South American state. It was rather the fact that the negotiations which settled the controversy laid the basis for the future attitude of the United States and Great Britain, not only toward each other, but toward the rest of the world. The immediate result of the controversy was also of significance. When the British Government agreed to enter into negotiations at Washington it thereby accepted the new interpretation of the Monroe Doctrine. This meant that the British had conceded to the demands of Secretary Olney and President Cleveland and in so doing had laid the foundation for the "durable friendship" which had been advocated by Mr. Chamberlain.

The first test of the "durable friendship" came with the election of 1896 and the free silver controversy. The currency question had been before the people con-

[32] *Ibid.*, p. 52.
[33] *Foreign Relations*, 1896, pp. 240-241, 247-255.

ce the adoption of the Bland silver act
In July, 1890, the Sherman silver law had
acted.   Three months later the McKinley
, closely associated with the silver question in
its   liate effect upon Anglo-American friendship,
was p. sed.   Both acts endangered Anglo-American
harmony, the former because it was supported by a
constituency which was opposed to a gold standard,
the latter because it advanced tariff rates.[34]

Following the enactment of those measures, American financial conditions became very complicated.
Poor crops, low prices, and social and industrial unrest
increased the difficulties.   New England manufacturers
and capitalists who were in constant touch with the
London money market desired the adoption of a gold
standard.   With the increase in the production of
silver in the West the ratio of value between gold
and silver had been disturbed.   This prompted the
silver producers to contend that a gold standard was
directly responsible for the low price of silver and
agricultural products.   As a result the western silver
producers and agriculturists demanded a system of
bimetallism in which a parity should be established
between the two metals.   The controversy which resulted seemed to threaten Anglo-American relations
seriously.   Vast sums of British capital had been invested in the development of American industry and
millions of dollars were advanced by the Americans
in gold, or its equivalent, in payment of the interest.
This led the silver forces to direct much criticism

[34] Cf. Parliamentary State Papers, Vol. CV, "Currency Correspondence," Enclosure 2 in No. II; New York Times, February 18, 1897.

against Great Britain whom they considered directly responsible for the maintenance of the gold standard on the London exchange. On the other hand, British and New England capitalists were of necessity greatly concerned, since the establishment of a silver standard in the United States would result in a decrease in the value of their property.

At the same time Europe, like the United States, was passing through a period of low prices, high interest rates, and industrial depression. This condition led banks and trust companies, as well as creditor nations, to call in gold reserves. In 1892, Austria-Hungary resumed specie payment and searched the money markets of the world for a gold redemption fund. In the same year Russia began to hoard gold for secret reasons, and France began to accumulate it to promote an increased note circulation. In 1893, due to natural financial caution and urged on by frequent bank failures, Great Britain began to strengthen her reserves. The result was that debtor nations and institutions found themselves deprived of not only all surplus gold but the necessary reserve funds as well. The United States, which had borrowed heavily, particularly from Great Britain, during the previous years of industrial expansion, was seriously concerned. Gold exports increased, money rates advanced and stocks fell. Domestic financial disorders, added to the foreign complications, produced the panic of 1893.

The apparent scarcity of gold on the market induced many Europeans to advocate bimetallism. In 1893 a momentary conference was held at Brussels with about twenty countries represented. Although the silver forces were defeated, predictions indicated that another conference would be held soon. The silver forces in the United States had followed the conference closely. As a result two questions arose among them: was it advisable to wait for European support or should they make the fight for bimetallism alone?

This difference of opinion led to much international bitterness. Germany, France, Great Britain, and the United States were generally considered as possessing sufficient financial prestige to control the world money market. Great Britain, as an extensive creditor nation, held the balance of power. As a creditor nation, however, she did not want bimetallism. In 1893 she gave proof of that by closing the Indian mints to the free coinage of silver. Immediately she became the recipient of the hatred of the American bimetallic forces. Furthermore, the British felt that certain Europeans, particularly the French and Germans, proposed to keep the good will of the American debtor classes by advocating bimetallism and at the same time to injure Great Britain by laying the failure of silver legislation upon her.[35]

On October 30, 1893, the Sherman silver act was finally repealed. The debate represented an effort of the seven silver mining states, a minority group, to block legislation and transfer political and economic power from the eastern capitalists to the western farmers and silver producers. Anti-British antipathy

[35] Cf. Parliamentary State Papers, Vol. CV, "Currency Correspondence," Enclosure 2 in No. II; New York Times, February 18, 1897.

was one of the weapons used.[36] Immediately after
their defeat in October, the silver forces began an
unprecedented educational campaign for votes. Again
anti-British prejudice became one of their tools. The
United States, they contended, was Great Britain's
most formidable rival in finance; nevertheless, she
was paying Great Britain two hundred million dollars
annually in gold in payment of interest on bonds.
To pay this interest the Americans sacrificed four
hundred million dollars in property, since silver was
worth only fifty cents on the dollar. In the impend-
ing struggle for the commercial mastery of the world,
a financial combat between the two countries could
not be avoided if the American people hoped to retain their own self-respect, freedom, and prosperity.
A war with England, said the "jingoes," would be
the most popular war ever waged.[37]

In May, 1895, the Harvey-Laughlin debate occurred
in Chicago. Mr. Harvey urged the danger of American financial dependence upon Great Britain. The
remedy he proposed was silver at the ratio of sixteen
to one. The result of such action would be to increase the cost of silver which Great Britain bought
from the American silver producers for use in her
Indian mints; advance the price of Indian wheat in

[36] *Congressional Record,* 53d Congress, 1st session, Vol. XXV, part 1,
pp. 400-411; *ibid.,* p. 1235; Stewart, William M., "Misrepresentation
of the Senate," *North American Review,* Vol. CLVII (November,
1893), pp. 513-522.

[37] For popular pamphlet arguments consult Harvey, William Hope,
Coin's Financial School (Chicago, 1894); *ibid., Tale of Two Nations*
(Chicago, 1894); White, Trumbull, *Silver and Gold* (Publisher's
Union, 1895).

proportion, reduce the value of gold and, as a result, advance the price of American fruit, wool, cotton, and silver bullion.[38] Mr. J. Lawrence Laughlin, who responded to Mr. Harvey, saw the currency question entirely apart from Anglo-American relations. In spite of Great Britain's wealth, the money market was controlled by the entire world and free silver would advance prices, lower wages, injure the debtor class, and produce silver monometallism.[39] Gold standard advocates uniformly agreed with Mr. Laughlin.[40]

Certain other influences combined to increase this hostility. The Democrats, who advocated a low tariff, accepted free silver with all its anti-British theories. Their platform for 1896 described gold monometallism as a British policy, both un-American and anti-American, which had brought other nations into financial servitude to London. The National Silver party and the Populists both declared a gold policy dangerous to American interests.[41] Besides this, it had been a Democratic government which had declared the new Monroe Doctrine and which had forced Venezuelan arbitration only a short time previously.

So far as the Republican party was concerned the British could hardly hope for more friendliness. Great Britain had never been disposed to look kindly upon the nomination of Mr. McKinley. As the originator of the tariff bill of 1890, they were inclined to look upon

[38] White, *Silver and Gold,* pp. 26-40.

[39] *Ibid.,* pp. 49-70.

[40] *Cf.* Roberts, George E., *Coin at School and in Finance* (Chicago, 1895).

[41] For a partial list of campaign speeches and the party platforms consult Bryan, William J., *The First Battle* (Chicago, 1896).

him as the champion of anti-British policies.[42] Furthermore, the Republicans had declared allegiance to protection and the new Monroe Doctrine. There was,
however, one great point of agreement—the Republicans were pledged to "sound mony" and "the existing gold standard" unless bimetallism should be
adopted by international agreement.

Finally order and Anglo-American harmony began
to emerge from this confusion of anti-British sentiment. In the first place, a few prominent British
thinkers comprehended the dual nature of the campaign probably better than the majority of Americans
did. They realized that the hostility of the silver forces
would cease with the return of financial prosperity.[43]
In the next place, John Hay, who held the confidence
of the members of the Coalition Government, visited
England during the summer of 1896. In a number of
confidential conversations with Mr. Balfour, Mr.
Chamberlain, Lord Curzon, and Sir William Harcourt,
Mr. Hay accomplished much toward retaining the
British friendship previously stimulated. The Republicans, he said, would sustain to the limit the action
of Mr. Cleveland concerning Venezuela and Mr. Mc-
Kinley was both a sound money man and friendly
toward Great Britain.[44] Furthermore, a few British

[42] *New York Tribune,* November 6, 8, 22, 1896.

[43] *Cf.* Shriver, Edwin J., "Silver Politics across Seas," *Westminster
Review,* Vol. CXLVI (November, 1896), pp. 487-495; *Spectator,*
July 4, 11, 1896.

[44] Thayer, William Roscoe, *The Life and Letters of John Hay,*
Vol. II (New York, 1915), pp. 143-144, 147, 150, 169. These conversations
were particularly significant since they marked the beginning of the
policy of the Opposition to overbid the party in power for American

leaders were in constant touch with certain prominent members of the Republican party. Senator Joseph B. Foraker had spent part of the summer in England and J. P. Morgan was in close association with the Rothschilds. Joseph Chamberlain and his wife, the daughter of William C. Endicott of Massachusetts, had visited in the United States. Finally, the papers generally read and quoted in London, were the three conservative New York dailies, each of which was uniformly fair, if not friendly, toward Great Britain.

What, then, was the effect of the currency struggle and the election of 1896 on Anglo-American relations? Great Britain was in a serious position throughout the controversy. Had the silver forces won in the United States the immediate loss to British capital would have run into the tens of millions of dollars and the consummation of any Anglo-American friendship would have been delayed for years. As it was, the thoughtful and considerate attitude shown by leading British statesmen and by the British newspapers revealed for the second time British friendship for the United States. Furthermore, with the defeat of free silver and the resumption of prosperity, which fortunately began soon after the election, the "jingoistic" hostility of the silver forces almost ceased. Indeed, it was always shallow and blustering in its nature, and

friendship. Two years later this policy had become so pronounced that Mr. Hay was led to urge upon Mr. Chamberlain the necessity for the party in power to state openly their attitude toward the United States in order to prevent the Americans from believing that the Opposition rather than the Government was friendly toward them. Mr. Chamberlain's speech at Birmingham on May 13, 1898, was the reply to Mr. Hay's request.

had exerted an influence out of proportion to its real significance. On the other hand, the good will promoted between the capitalists and manufacturers of Great Britain and the United States through the recognition of their common financial interests, was of considerable significance in creating common Anglo-American commercial policies.

Throughout almost the entire time that the interest of the United States and Great Britain had been directed toward the Venezuelan boundary controversy, the currency question and the election of 1896, a few individuals, both British and American, sought to find some method by which war might in the future be eliminated between the two countries. On March 5, 1896, the British proposed a treaty of arbitration. Although it received the sincere support of both Mr. Olney and Mr. Cleveland, nothing was gained.[45] Sentiment, however, grew steadily stronger in favour of arbitration and on January 11, 1897, just three weeks before the conclusion of the treaty which sent the Venezuelan boundary controversy to arbitration, Mr. Olney and Sir Julian Pauncefote, the British ambassador at Washington, signed a general treaty of arbitration. On the same day President Cleveland sent it to the Senate, with an earnest request for its favourable consideration.[46]

The press, the pulpit, the colleges and universities, and the business world generally favoured the treaty.[47]

[45] *Foreign Relations*, 1896, pp. 222-237.

[46] *Ibid.*, pp. 237-240.

[47] *London Times*, January 12, 14, 16, 1897; *New York Times*, January 12, 13, 14, 15, 16, 23, 1897; *New York Herald*, January 12, 14, 1897; The *Sun* was the only prominent New York paper adverse.

On January 14, opposition was first reported in the Senate. Next, the anti-British elements in the United States, having learned that both Lord Salisbury and the British people were extremely anxious for the early ratification of the treaty, argued that there must be some sinister motive back of it and they began to fight it.[48] On January 19, Mr. Olney appeared before the Senator committee on foreign relations in behalf of the treaty. Immediately a few senators began to argue against "coercion" from the state department. Besides this, they disliked Lord Pauncefote.[49] After February 1, the fight for the treaty became hopeless and on February 18, the treaty was turned over to the Republican administration.[50] On March 18, the treaty went to the Senate once more, where the contest continued with considerable bitterness until May 5, when it was voted down by a vote of forty-three to twenty-six.[51] The causes for the defeat of the bill were numerous and conflicting. A minority in the Senate objected to what they considered coercion from the state department and the general public.[52]

[48] London Times, January 14, 20, 1897.

[49] Smalley, George W., Anglo-American Memories (London, 1912), p. 178.

[50] New York Times, January 23, February 11, 1897; London Times, February 2, 15, 1897; Annual Register, 1897 (new series), part 1, p. 386.

[51] The vote was divided with thirty Republicans and ten Democrats in the affirmative and ten Republicans, eleven Democrats, and five Populists in the negative. For a British analysis of the votes consult London Times, May 7, 1897.

[52] Out of nearly 250 petitions presented in the Senate carrying signatures varying in number from several thousand to one, only fifteen were in opposition. Of those fifteen the majority were from organizations with a membership largely Irish. The New York Times,

Some senators felt that it would force the Senate to yield up its constitutional function as a part of the treaty-making power.[53] Some preferred that all questions should be approved by the Senate before sending them to arbitration.[54] Others "thought they were striking a blow at the chief gold standard nation." [55] Senator Morgan of Alabama was accused of opposing arbitration until the government should pass the hundred million dollar Nicaragua canal bond.

The outcome of the treaty contest was the moral equivalent of a victory for the development of Anglo-American good will. It proved to Great Britain that many of the American people, the press, the church, and the President favoured British friendship. One tragedy grew out of its defeat. Sir Julian Pauncefote and Mr. Olney had begun the work on the treaty "as a labour of love." Into its development Sir Julian had crowded the thought and energy of years of work, for he loved the American people next to his own. The failure of the Senate to ratify the treaty came

January 23, 1897, reported Senator George F. Hoar as saying, "I hold this meddling with important diplomacy by angry and impassioned utterances mischievous and foolish." Senator Shelby Cullom was supposed to agree with Mr. Hoar; *New York Times*, January 27, 1897, "The whip and spur of public opinion ought to be applied mercilessly" since one motive for delay is the hostility toward the President and the Secretary of State.

[53] *New York Times*, February 10, 1897.

[54] *London Times*, March 19, 1897.

[55] *New York Times*, May 7, 1897—with very few exceptions the twenty-six Senators who voted against ratification were free silver men. Party politics counted for little or nothing. It was a free silver and anti-Cleveland vote that killed the treaty. Race hostility to England may have influenced Senator Murphy who represented the state of New York in the Senate. Silver was the main thing.

as his first great disappointment. Indeed, so serious
was his feeling of defeat that his health was permanently impaired.

Beginning almost immediately after the inaugura-
tion of President McKinley there followed a series
of events which may be described not inaccurately
as the era of Anglo-American good will of 1897. The
first of these was found in the unqualified assurances
of American friendship which had been brought out
during the debate on the general treaty of arbitration. The second of these was the appointment of
John Hay as ambassador to Great Britain. Probably
no other American has ever held the confidence and
respect of the British government and people as he
did. Happy in the English environment of culture
and refinement he became at once the champion of
Anglo-American amity. ". . . the dearest wish of my
heart," he said, "is that the happy relations now
subsisting between the two great nations may be not
only continued, but if possible, drawn closer together
during the time that I shall hold the office of ambassador." [56] In all probability Mr. Hay was responsible for the elimination of more Anglo-American
prejudice than any other man of the century. Cultured, capable, and tactful he brought to the British
people all that was best in American manhood and
statesmanship.

Following closely upon the appointment of Mr.

[56] Hay, John, *Addresses of John Hay* (New York, 1907), pp. 63-65.
For the British attitude toward Mr. Hay consult *London Times,*
February 22, March 3, 1897; *New York Times,* January 7, March 3,
1897.

Hay came the third event of interest. The *Log of the Mayflower* or the *Bradford Manuscript* had been in England for many years. No less than four attempts had been made to secure possession of it. Finally through the efforts of Senator George F. Hoar and the Archbishop of Canterbury, Queen Victoria secured the authorization for its return in the care of Mr. Bayard. Speaking later of this act Senator Hoar said, ". . . the restoration of this priceless manuscript did more to cement the bonds of friendship between the people of the two countries than forty canal treaties. In settling Imperial questions both nations are thinking, properly and naturally, of great interests. But this restoration was an act of purest kindness." [57]

In June, Great Britain planned to celebrate the Diamond Jubilee of Queen Victoria. Mr. Hay recognized the importance of America's part in that event and, largely through his efforts, made it an occasion for a display of mutual friendliness. The army and navy were represented with detachments under the command of Admiral Joseph N. Miller and General Nelson A. Miles. Mr. Whitelaw Reid was made ambassador extraordinary on special mission. Mr. John Sherman, secretary of state, sent a formal note of congratulation on the Queen's birthday. This was followed four days later by an informal note over the personal signature of President McKinley. The tact, good will, and genuine friendship of the note touched not only the emotion of the Queen but all England.

[57] Hoar, George F., *Autobiography of Seventy Years* (London, 1904), Vol. II, pp. 247-251.

British papers copied it, commented upon it, and praised it.[58]

Throughout the United States Jubilee services were held in all Episcopal churches with special ritual prepared for the occasion. In many of the churches, particularly of the East, Jubilee services were held regardless of denomination. Of the large cities of the country celebrations were held in San Francisco, Chicago, St. Louis, Boston, Kansas City, and New York. A number of the leading pupits of London were occupied by American preachers, all of whom delivered Jubilee addresses. The general decorations for the churches were a mingling of the British and American flags. The British National Anthem was always sung.[59]

Scores of messages of congratulation were sent by American commercial organizations. The Chamber of Commerce of the state of New York sent congratulations. The New York Exchange sent greetings to

[58] "Great and Good Friend: In the name and behalf of the people of the United States, I present their sincere felicitations upon the sixtieth anniversary of Your Majesty's accession to the Crown of Great Britain. I express the sentiments of my fellow-citizens in wishing for your people the prolongation of a reign illustrious and marked by advance in science, arts, and popular well-being. On behalf of my countrymen, I wish particularly to recognize your friendship for the United States, and your love of peace, exemplified upon important occasions. It is pleasing to acknowledge the debt of gratitude and respect due to your personal virtues. May your life be prolonged, and peace, honor, and prosperity bless the people over whom you have been called to rule. May liberty flourish throughout your Empire, under just and equal laws, and your Government continue strong in the affections of all who live under it. And I pray God to have Your Majesty in His holy keeping." It was signed simply "Your good friend, William McKinley." *Foreign Relations*, 1897, p. 252.

[59] *New York Tribune*, June 20, 1897.

the London Stock Exchange. The New York Cotton Exchange sent greetings to the Liverpool Cotton Association. The dominant note of all the messages was the desire that the feeling of friendship between the two nations be permanent.[60]

On the arrival of the American mission nothing was left undone that might show favour or give pleasure. Two things impressed Mr. Reid most: the great devotion shown to the Queen and "the obvious and continuous cordiality toward America." [61] During the procession the Americans received almost continuous applause.[62] Entire columns were given in the British papers to appreciation of the interest of the United States in the celebration, her love for the Queen, her good will toward Canada and her friendship for Great Britain.[63]

The effect of the Jubilee upon Anglo-American relations was significant. It had afforded an opportunity for the free and open expression of international good will. It served to give confidence to the Canadians in their relation to the United States. It showed that the bad spirit stirred up by the Venezuelan controversy, the currency struggle and the election of 1896 was gone. And, finally, it showed that the Americans, in spite of their national independence, were profoundly proud of their racial inheritance.

Throughout the year other incidents, perhaps in-

[60] *Cf. New York Times,* June 20, 21, 22, 1897; *New York Tribune,* June 20, 21, 22, 1897.

[61] Cortissoz, Royal, *The Life of Whitelaw Reid* (New York, 1921), p. 216.

[62] *Ibid.,* p. 216.

[63] *London Times,* June 21, 22, 23, 1897.

significant in themselves, revealed the growing Anglo-American harmony. Only a few can be mentioned.

On March 10, occurred the formal presentation of the diplomatic corps to the President. The body was headed by Sir Julian Pauncefote as doyen. Contrary to custom a short conversation ensued when President McKinley greeted Sir Julian, in which the former expressed his appreciation of the services he had rendered with respect to the arbitration treaty. Sir Julian responded by congratulating the President on his election and his inaugural address. The incident marked the beginning of a sincere friendship between the two. The incident was but the first of a series in which Mr. McKinley gave full assurance of his respect and friendship for the British nation.[64]

In June, 1897, speaking at Nashville, Mr. McKinley said, "The builders of this State brought with them the same high ideals and fearless devotion to home and country, founded upon resistance to oppression, which have ever made illustrious the Anglo-American name." Two British comments followed. "The jingoes will not like his phrase. It may be taken as a mark of the President's sincere good will for the mother country." [65]

By the close of October it is safe to say that Mr. McKinley had secured the confidence of the British party in power. He had accomplished this through the work of Mr. Hay, through his sincere coöperation

[64] *London Times,* March 12, 1897; *New York Times,* March 11, 1897.
[65] *London Times,* June 12, 1897; See *London Times,* October 31, 1897; *New York Times,* October 31, 1897, for comments on Mr. McKinley's speech before the Commercial Club at Cincinnati, October 30.

in the Jubilee, his letter to the Queen, his pronouncement of Anglo-American ideals, his preference for Sir Julian and arbitration and his good will toward Great Britain generally. In their friendship for Mr. McKinley, the British openly recognized the conflict between the Senate and the President as head of the department of state. The Senate and John Sherman, as they saw it, had killed arbitration in opposition to Mr. McKinley and the will of the people. "People," said the *London Times* of April 4, 1897, "have ceased to expect the Senate to acquire the art of minding its own business."

Assurance of British confidence in American friendliness and in sound money came in this way. Immediately after the election of Mr. McKinley, Mr. E. O. Walcott went to Europe in the interests of bimetallism. The French and Germans were open in their offers of coöperation but everything was made dependent upon Great Britain's opening the Indian mints. This, of course, she would not do. Negotiations continued until September 16, 1897, when the Indian office recommended rejection of the proposals. On October 19, Lord Salisbury forwarded its decision to the American Government. The announcement caused hardly a ripple of comment in the United States.

CHAPTER IV

GREAT BRITAIN AND THE BEGINNING OF THE WAR WITH SPAIN

EARLY in 1897 it was apparent that the Cuban revolution had assumed an international significance. In the last days of 1896 Spain had refused the joint request of France, Great Britain, and Germany that she should accept the good offices of the United States with a view to assuring a prompt termination of the war. As a result of this joint action, however, she had published, on February 6, 1897, a decree which granted Cuba a reformed system of government to go into operation as soon as the state of war in Cuba would permit.[1]

This decree served only to complicate the situation.[2] The insurgents were steadily growing more determined in their demands for independence, while Spain was equally resolved that no amelioration of Cuban conditions should be granted until the parties demanding the reforms should put themselves at her mercy by throwing down their arms. The insurgents felt that Spain's promise was worthless,[3] that nothing

[1] Chadwick, French Ensor, *The Relations of the United States and Spain, Diplomacy* (New York, 1909), p. 487; *Chicago Daily Inter Ocean*, February 6, 1897.

[2] *Inter Ocean*, February 7, 1897.

[3] *Pall Mall Gazette*, February 5, 1897.

short of complete independence could now be accepted.[4]

The projected reforms received much critical comment both in the United States and in Great Britain. In the United States many considered them merely as a subterfuge to divert American interest until General Weyler had completed his conquest of the island.[5] Others felt that the reforms had been offered in good faith and that they granted all that could reasonably be expected.[6] In British comment the proposed reforms were generally spoken of as a dead letter. Public opinion was unanimous in considering them unavailing for the purpose of terminating the war.[7]

Following the February decree the insurrection became, on the part of Spain, a war of annihilation or complete subjection. Immediately American sentiment began to respond to the situation for both humanitarian and commercial reasons.[8] In March the Republican party came into power, pledged to secure peace and independence in Cuba. On May 24, a bill was passed and approved by the President appropriating fifty thousand dollars for the relief and transporta-

[4] Cf. Chadwick, Relations of the United States and Spain, pp. 487-488; Inter Ocean, February 10, 1897, contained an interview granted by Maximo Gomez to its correspondent on January 31. It is difficult to determine when the insurgents became united in their demands for independence but it was probably between January 8 and January 31. Cf. Pall Mall Gazette, January 8, 16, 17, 1897.

[5] Callahan, James Morton, Cuba and International Relations (Baltimore, 1899), p. 472.

[6] Chadwick, op. cit., pp. 487-488; Pall Mall Gazette, January 8, 1897.

[7] London Times, February 2, 1897.

[8] Inter Ocean, February 26, March 2, 3, 1897; Congressional Record, Vol. XXIX, part 3, 54th Congress, 2d session, p. 2287.

tion of suffering 'American citizens in the island of Cuba.[9] On June 26, the secretary of state, John Sherman, in a note to Dupuy de Lome, the Spanish minister at Washington, issued a protest against the Spanish policy of 'devastation and reconcentration in Cuba.[10] On September 13, General Stewart L. Woodford succeeded Hannis Taylor as American minister at Spain. Ten days later he presented a note to the Spanish court setting forth the views of the McKinley administration on the Cuban situation and tendering the services of the United States once more in an effort to secure peace.[11] Six days later the conservative ministry of Cánovas del Castillo resigned to be succeeded on October 14 by the liberal ministry of Praxedes Mateo Sagasta. On October 17, General Don Raymon y Erenas Blanco was appointed as governor and captain-general of Cuba.

Throughout the earlier part of the year the British press followed the Cuban situation with keen interest.[12] General Weyler y Nicolau was condemned as a soldier and declared incompetent as a civil administrator.[13] Mr. McKinley's determination to form his own plans and keep them conservative was fully respected and approved.[14] His opposition, it was contended, did not come from the American people but from the Senate.

[9] *United States Statutes at Large*, Vol. XXX, 55th Congress, 1st session, p. 520.

[10] *Foreign Relations of the United States*, 1897, pp. 507-508.

[11] *Ibid.*, 1898, pp. 568-573.

[12] *The Pall Mall Gazette* and *London Times* commented almost daily on the Cuban situation.

[13] *London Times*, January 4, 1897.

[14] *Ibid.*, May 20, 1897.

It was a continuation of the same struggle which Mr. Cleveland had waged with his Senate.[15] Silver and Cuban "jingoism" were 'associated together in some vague way on the theory that war would force the United States on a silver basis.[16]

Generally speaking, the British Government understood and approved of 'the Cuban policy advanced by the President. This sympathetic reaction was probably due to two facts: as an Anglo-Saxon nation she could interpret Anglo-Saxon motives, and she hoped to receive in return an expression of American interest in British affairs in Europe.[17] On September 13, Mr. Woodford was received by the Queen of Spain and presented his letters of credence. Five days previous to this Sir Henry Drummond Wolff, the British ambassador, called upon Mr. Woodford. A "friendly interview" followed, in which the American minister outlined the Cuban situation carefully. Mr. Woodford first assured Sir Henry that the United States desired neither to annex Cuba nor to establish a protectorate over the island. He then mentioned various respects in which the United States was closely associated with Cuba. Nearly every epidemic of yellow fever in the United States had originated in Havana or at some point in Cuba, from which the disease had

[15] *Ibid.*, May 20, 1897.

[16] *Ibid.*, May 20, 1897; *British Weekly,* November 11, 1897.

[17] Beginning in the early days of January, 1898, the *New York Herald* published extracts from British newspapers on the average of not less than twice a week, setting forth American interests in China and their similarity to British interests. Among the British papers emphasizing the similarity of interests were the *London Times, Pall Mall Gazette, Daily News, Statist* and the *British Weekly.*

spread to the American coast. Cuban sugar was as
vital to America as the wheat and cotton of India
and Egypt were to Great Britain. The war had in-
flicted great pecuniary losses on the American people.
Exports and imports had declined heavily. He next
mentioned the fact that, although Spain had early
acknowledged the belligerency of the South in the recent Civil War, the United States had consistently
for thirteen years observed all the obligations of neutrality. Next he told Sir Henry something "of the hor-
rible and unchristian and uncivilized manner in which
the present struggle in Cuba" was carried on. Then
he "put the direct question to him whether, if Cuba
lay about 100 miles west of the United Kingdom, and
if all the conditions existed therein and between Cuba
and the United Kingdom which now exist in Cuba
and between Cuba and the United States, England
would not be compelled in the interest of her people
and of humanity and of civilization to find some way
of putting promptly an end to the struggle?" He
proposed no remedy for the situation other than that
some means of restoring peace must be found before
Congress met in December. He assured Sir Henry
that not only had the Spanish government failed to
repress the rebellion but that the rebellion was stronger
than ever. He concluded by saying that the United
States stood ready to offer her services in an effort to
restore peace and that should Spain see fit to offer
"without any evasion or reservation" such autonomy
as Great Britain granted Canada there would be a
reasonable certainty of Cuban peace and prosperity.[18]

[18] *Foreign Relations*, 1898, pp. 562-565.

A summary of this conversation was forwarded immediately to Lord Salisbury. It represented the first authoritative or official statement that Great Britain had received from the United States on the Cuban question.

On September 14, Mr. Woodford reported his conversation with the Spanish minister to John Sherman. At the same time he set forth his relations with the British embassy. "He [Mr. Wolff] has received me with very prompt and exceedingly generous and hospitable welcome, and I trust and believe that the relations between our legation and the British embassy will continue upon the same friendly and cordial relations as heretofore. No effort on my part shall be wanting to secure this most desirable result." [19]

The earnest desire of the Spanish Government to meet the demands of the United States was shown on October 6, when the order for General Weyler's recall was given. On October 31, General Blanco succeeded as governor-general of Cuba. Immediately he began a campaign to relieve the suffering of reconcentration. It was without result, however, for the American consuls continued to report the conditions daily observed, as beyond belief.[20]

[19] *Ibid.*, p. 565. On January 30, 1899, the *Pall Mall Gazette* quoted Mr. Woodford as saying that ". . . had it not been for the unfaltering, unchanging, and loyal friendship of England, and the attitude of her minister in Madrid, I might have failed to do the little I did do because the representatives in Madrid of Continental Europe were ready at any time to interfere with the plans of the United States, if the British Minister would only join them." This was taken from Mr. Woodford's speech given before the Army and Navy Club in New York on Saturday, January 28, 1899.

[20] Chadwick, *The Relations of the United States and Spain*, p. 522.

On November 23, the Queen Regent granted autonomy to the Cubans subject to the consent of the Cortes. Both 'the United States and Great Britain recognized this as entirely inadequate to meet the Cuban demands, since at different times throughout the year they had called attention to the different interpretations placed on colonial autonomy by Anglo-Saxon and Spanish officials.[21] It was in the former sense that the Cubans understood it.

Throughout the early months of 1898 the British press followed the rumours of a Spanish-American war assiduously. On February 9, the Cuban Junta gave the Dupuy de Lome letter to the press. One paragraph of it revealed de Lome's distorted interpretation of Anglo-American events. "I do not believe you [the Spanish] pay enough attention to the rôle of England. To my mind the only object of England is that Americans should occupy themselves with us and leave her in peace, and if there is a war, so much the better, for that would further remove what is threatening her, although that will never come." [22] In all probability Mr. de Lome felt that Great Britain was endangered by American commercial expansion and that a war with Spain would serve to cripple the United States and enable Great Britain to maintain her own prestige.

The British press, throughout, chose to ignore the reference to Great Britain's interest in American affairs

[21] *London Times,* February 9, 12, October 10, 1898; *Northern Trade and Finance,* December 15, 1897; *Foreign Relations,* 1898, p. 522; *Statist,* March 19, 1898.

[22] *Public Opinion,* February 17, 1898.

in Cuba, but condemned the letter unreservedly as a violation of the ethics of international diplomacy.[23] This attitude was highly acceptable to the American press. On February 14, the London correspondent of the *New York Tribune* wrote thus: "English comments on the Spanish minister's breach of international etiquette have been inspired by a sense of justice and a spirit of good-will toward the United States. Nearly every journal describes the letter as an unpardonable outrage." It is a new thing to find the English journals cordial and outspoken in their admiration of Mr. McKinley. "There is a change of temper and spirit which can only be explained as a direct effect of American expressions of respect and good-will toward England on the Chinese question. One good turn deserves another; the American press was just to England and the English press is now equally fair to America."

Hardly had the British press ceased to comment on the de Lome incident when the U.S.S. *Maine* was sunk in the harbour of Havana on February 15. On the following day Sir Julian Pauncefote called on President McKinley to express his regret over the disaster. Throughout February 16 and 17, numerous messages of sympathy came from Great Britain. Among those sending them were the Queen, the Prince and Princess

---

[23] *London Times,* February 11, 1898, "It is from every point of view deplorable and lamentable that so useful a career [that of de Lome] should have been terminated by an act of basest treachery." The *London Telegraph,* February 11, 1898, declared the letter hardly "consonant" even as a private letter, "with a tenure of a high diplomatic post." The *Statist,* February 12, 1898, called it "merely an unpleasant diplomatic incident." *Cf. Literary Digest,* March 12, 1898; *Public Opinion,* February 18, 1898; *Spectator,* February 12, 1898.

of Wales, the Duke of Connaught, Lord Mayor of
London, the Earl of Aberdeen, Governor General of
Canada, the Duke and Duchess of York, N. M. Roths-
child and Sons, and many others. Sir Algernon Borth-
wick, owner of the *Morning Post,* asked to be allowed
to open subscriptions in his newspaper for the relief
of the families of those lost in the *Maine.*[24] The
British journals of February 16 expressed profound sor-
row. The headlines of the evening papers hinted at
treachery, either Cuban or Spanish. The morning
papers of February 17 commented very soberly but
complimented the United States on the good sense,
good feeling and dignity exhibited.[25] Sympathy with
the American government will be world-wide, said
the *London Times,* "but nowhere will the feeling be
so general or profound as amongst their British and
Irish kinsfolks at home and in the colonies."[26] Gradually an appreciation of this spirit of British sympathy
spread throughout the United States leaving a new
and enlarged feeling of good will as it went.[27]

After the sinking of the *Maine,* Great Britain was
convinced that war was imminent between Spain and
the United States.[28] Gradually it had become apparent to her that in the event of such a war France,
Germany, and Austria would extend their sympathy if

[24] *Foreign Relations,* 1898, pp. 1054-58.

[25] *St. James Budget,* March 25, 1898; *London Times,* February 17,
1898; *Pall Mall Gazette,* February 17, 18, 1898; *Foreign Relations,*
1898, pp. 1054-58.

[26] *London Times,* February 17, 1898.

[27] *New York Times,* February 25, 1898; *Public Opinion,* February
18, 1898.

[28] *Statist,* February 19, 1898.

not their actual aid to Spain. At the same time, Great Britain realized that she herself faced the possibility of an alliance of France, Germany, and Russia in the East.[29]

Out of these complications there developed a diversity of rumours both in the United States and in Great Britain indicative of the growing appreciation and association of Anglo-American interests. On March 8, Sir Julian Pauncefote, accompanied by the American secretary of state, visited President McKinley. Whatever may have been the object of his visit, the conjecture immediately arose that he carried a message of good will from the British Government.[30] "America fully believes," reported the *London Times*, "that she has England's moral support in the policy of which she accepts the President as exponent." [31]

On March 10, the rumour became current in Great Britain that in case of an emergency the British fleet might show itself as a friend on the American coasts.[32] On the same day, in the House of Commons, Sir James Fergusson asked Mr. G. N. Curzon, as representative of the Government, whether his attention had been called to telegraphic reports as to alleged communications on the Cuban question between the British ambassador at Washington and the United States Government; and whether there was any truth in those

[29] *Cf. Parliamentary Debates of the United Kingdom of Great Britain and Ireland* (Hansard's), Vol. LIV, pp. 1252, 1342.

[30] *New York Times*, March 9, 1898.

[31] *London Times*, March 9, 1898.

[32] *London Times*, March 10, 1898; *New York Times*, March 11, 1898. This rumour was sometimes referred to as the Des Voeux suggestion.

reports. Mr. Curzon replied that there was no truth in the report, that no communications on the Cuban question had passed between the British and the United States Governments.[33]

On March 10, Pauncefote made another call on the President. While they were in conference, they were joined by the Japanese minister. As a result, the evening papers carried reports of the possibility of a triple alliance. Even Parliament was moved. Mr. H. V. Duncombe, M.P., was reported as saying that the opinion was widely held in the House that foreign powers should be told that a blow struck at either England or the United States was a blow at the other.[34]

By the middle of March, Great Britain began to realize that the United States would be forced to enter Cuba because of humanitarian motives.[35] The principal factor that was operating for peace was the policy of "firmness, caution, and pacific circumspection" which President McKinley pursued in regard to foreign affairs. In that policy he was sup-

[33] *Hansard's Parliamentary Debates*, Vol. LIV, pp. 1243-1244.

[34] *London Times*, March 11, 1898; *New York Times*, March 11, 1898; *Chronicle*, March 19, gave the story of this incident. On Thursday of last week, Mr. Duncombe asked "whether, in the event of complications between the United States and a foreign Power, the British fleet would not be put at this country's [United States] service." The propounder was allowed to withdraw the question. The question met with no rebuke, however. (This explains why the incident does not occur in Hansard's.)

[35] "The Spanish Crisis," *Blackwood's Magazine*, Vol. CLXIII (February, 1898), pp. 238-253; *Spectator*, March 14, 1898; "The United States and Spain," *Quarterly Review*, Vol, CLXXXVIII (July, 1898), pp. 216-241; *Statist*, March 26, 1898; *Graphic*, March 5, 1898 contains a number of illustrations showing terrible poverty existing among the Cubans.

ported by the "sober and conscientious mass of the American people." [36]

On March 14, rumours of an Anglo-American alliance again reached Parliament when Michael Davitt asked the Under Secretary of State for War whether any British war vessels were to be loaned to the American government in case of war between that republic and any European power. Mr. W. St. John Brodrick replied in the negative.[37] Not yet satisfied, Mr. Davitt immediately asked the Under Secretary of State for Foreign Affairs if Lord Pauncefote had made proposals to the United States for an alliance between the two governments in the event of serious complications arising out of present difficulties in the Far East; if similar proposals had been tendered by President McKinley to the British government; or if offers of mediation between the United States and Spain in the relation to Cuban troubles had been made from "exalted quarters" in England to President McKinley. Lord Curzon replied that the character of the questions was such that it would be inexpedient for him to reply to them.[38]

On March 17, Senator Redfield Proctor of Vermont reported in the Senate on his unofficial visit to Cuba.[39] The speech aroused considerable attention. The *London Times* after commenting on the integrity of the witness called the speech the one incident, if there was one, not making for peace. "He avoids exaggeration and emotion, even inference, and his statement

[35] *London Times,* March 8, 1898; *Statist,* March 26, 1898.

[37] *Hansard's Parliamentary Debates,* Vol. LIV, p. 1526.

[38] *Ibid.,* p. 1526.

[39] *Congressional Record,* Vol. XXXI, part 3, 55th Congress, 2d session, pp. 2916-2918.

tells heavily for intervention or mediation for the rescue of Cuba from an impossible situation." [40]

Throughout March the United States and Great Britain began to recognize the unanimity of Continental opinion in favour of Spain.[41] The Austrian and French Governments expressed open sympathy for her.[42] In Germany many of the people and some of the unofficial journals supported her. Outwardly, at least, however, the German Government expressed full neutrality. Commercial interests, as well as regard for the German-Americans and for international expediency, demanded this.[43]

On March 28, President McKinley forwarded the report of the naval court of inquiry on the *Maine* disaster to Congress. This address represented his last attempt to prevent war, and Great Britain noted it with intense interest. The *Times* maintained that peace was still in his hands. "We may yet be saved from the sad spectacle of a contest between two friendly nations both bound to us by the bonds of an old friendship, though, should the worst come to the worst, we shall not of course forget, whilst maintaining the duties of neutrality towards both, that one of them is knotted to us more closely by the ties of blood." [44] The *Statist* spoke of the message as "admirable in tone." Its effect would be to calm public

[40] *London Times,* March 19, 24; *Pall Mall Gazette,* March 19, 1898; *Public Opinion,* March 24, 1898.

[41] *New York Times,* March 22, 1898; *London Times,* March 15, 1898.

[42] *Public Opinion,* March 17, 1898.

[43] *London Times,* March 21, 1898.

[44] *London Times,* March 28, 1898.

excitement and assure Spain that the measure of autonomy already granted the Cubans was entirely insufficient. The message, it said, was received in the United States with a calmness that was honourable to the American people.[45]

On the following day, March 29, British interest reached unprecedented heights. "It must be admitted that, with every desire to excuse the reluctance of Spain to yield to pressure . . . we cannot refuse our sympathy to the people of the United States in circumstances which would have made it difficult even for our own countrymen to preserve their boasted calm." The relation between the two countries is not, and ought not to be, one of sentiment only. "The two great English-speaking communities have immense, permanent, and increasing interests in common, and recent events have strongly illustrated this community of interests in the Far East. Commerce and civilization in those lands and seas mean far more to the English and the Americans, who were the first to open them up to western intercourse, than they can possibly mean to Powers which look immediately and chiefly for political domination and which do not understand the policy of the open door."[46] The same day Alfred Austin, British poet laureate, published his poem, "A Voice from the West," on an Anglo-American alliance.[47] It was cabled to the *New York*

[45] *Statist,* April 2, 1898.
[46] *London Times,* March 29, 1898.
[47] "What is the voice I hear
    On the winds of the western sea?
Sentinel, listen, from out Cape Clear
And say what the voice may be.

Herald and appeared simultaneously in that journal and in the *London Times*.

Throughout the earlier part of April, while Great Britain's situation in the East was growing darker,

> 'Tis a proud free people calling loud
> to a people proud and free.
>
> "And it says to them: 'Kinsmen, hail;
> We severed have been too long.
> Now let us have done with a worn-out tale—
> The tale of ancient wrong—
> And our friendship last long as our love doth last,
> and be stronger than death is strong.'
>
> "Answer then, sons of the self-same race,
> And blood of the self-same clan;
> Let us speak with each other face to face
> And answer as man to man,
> And loyally love and trust each other as
> none but free men can.
>
> "Now fling them out to the breeze,
> Shamrock, Thistle, and Rose,
> And the Star-spangled Banner unfurl with these—
> A message to friends and foes
> Wherever the sails of peace are seen and
> wherever the war wind blows—
>
> "A message to bond and thrall to wake,
> For whenever we come, we twain,
> The throne of the tyrant shall rock and quake,
> And this menace be void and vain,
> For you are lords of a strong land and we
> are lords of the main.
>
> "Yes, this is the voice of the bluff March gale;
> We severed have been too long;
> But now we have done with a worn-out tale—
> The tale of an ancient wrong—
> And our friendship shall last as love doth last
> and be stronger than death is strong."

America's situation in Cuba was likewise clouding. In both cases the common enemies included Germany and France, though Russia, an enemy of Great Britain, was still looked upon with favour by many in the United States. The manufacturing interests of the United States, however, had become by this time quite generally conscious of America's relation to Great Britain's foreign policy. On April 4, the *New York Times* declared that it was a pity that the American State Department had been unable to force American assistance for Great Britain in the Far East. In May the British *Review of Reviews* indicated the growing commercial relation of the two Powers in a parody by "Ouida" on "A Voice from the West," entitled, "A Voice from the Sea." [48]

[48] "What is the voice I hear
O'er the wires of the Western Sea?
'Stockbroker! Listen from Mincing Lane
And say what the voice may be!'
' 'Tis the voice of Pharisee people, calling loud
To a People as Pharisee!'

"And one says to t'other,
'Old man! We've growl'd and scowl'd too long;
We haven't seen our interests right,
We both know we can't do wrong;
We both love swagger and rot,
Alone, each can lick Creation; together
we'll give it 'em hot!

"We're brothers, like Cain and Abel;
We're friends, like the cat and the dog;
But we'll boom the self-same paper,
And we'll roll the self-same log;
For the same blood runs in our veins—oh, my eyes!
lestways, when it t'aint otherwise!

Throughout the first week of April, war spirit developed rapidly.[49]   On April 5, Mr. Woodford notified Secretary Sherman that, in view of the very critical relations between Spain and the United States, he had asked the British *chargé d'affaires* at Madrid to assume charge of American interests in Spain.[50]   The following day representatives of the six Powers, Great Britain, Germany, France, Austria-Hungary, Russia, and Italy, addressed a note to the American government in behalf of peace.[51]   Two days later the *London Times* explained that Great Britain's signature to the peace note was in no way hostile to the United

> "So fling 'em out on the breeze
>   Bluster, and Bully, and Brag!
> And the standard of Spangled Shoddy
>   Shall wave o'er a Sea of Swag,
> Wherever the Press shall vapour and
>   wherever the Purse shall wag.
>
> "For wherever we come, we twain,
>   The machine gun shall bellow of Jesus,
> And the Bible preach gin and gain,
>   For our greed and gospel's the same.
> And if we've made an end of the Redskin,
>   so have you of his Maori kin.
>
> " 'Yes; this is the voice on the bluff March gale;
>   We've squabbled and sniggered too long,
> But now we'll tell quite another tale
>   And on 'Change sing another song.
> We'll smoke our pipes together,
>   long as our baccy'll hold,
> And face the dirty weather
>   safe in each other's gold.' "

[49] *Pall Mall Gazette,* April 4, 6, 1898.
[50] *Foreign Relations,* 1898, pp. 739-740.
[51] *Ibid.,* pp. 740-741.

States. On April 19, rumour that the United States had resented this action as unwarrantable interference with her responsibilities was considered in the House of Commons.[52]

Early in the winter of 1902 these last efforts to secure peace led to the final attempt on the part of Germany to discredit the friendship which Great Britain had extended to the United States during the Spanish American War. The Kaiser ordered a racing yacht to be built in the United States. Later, he decided to send Prince Henry on an unofficial visit to be present at the launching of the boat. Miss Alice Roosevelt was asked to christen it. Both the German and the American press made much of the proposed visit. The British, unwisely, considered the situation with alarm, feeling that it might endanger the Anglo-American friendship. In all probability the British press went too far in their protestations of friendship for the United States, since the German press saw fit to retaliate. On February 6, the *New York Times* published what appeared to be a semi-official report. "Almost exactly four years ago the Spanish ambassador here asked Germany whether Germany would lead in action against the United States for the protection of the monarchial principles. The answer was a definite refusal, and the same was given a month later, about the middle of March, when the invitation reached Germany to participate in the intervention undertaken upon the initiative of Austria. . . . After that, several attempts were made to induce Germany, or the Dreibund, to agree to intervention, in which attempts the Pope was especially active. The final result was that Dr. von Holleben, German ambassador to Washington, was instructed to join in the steps proposed by Austria only in case all the other five great Powers participated." The article continued that on April 7, a collective note, signed by the six Powers, was handed to the officials at Washington, advising a peaceable settlement. On April 14, Great Britain, through her ambassador, proposed a new collective note, in which the Powers should declare that Europe regarded America's armed intervention in Cuba as unjustifiable. The ambassadors telegraphed to their home governments asking for instructions. The step failed through Germany's refusal. "Afterwards, in June and July, while the United States was making great progress in the Philippines, England actively tried to induce the Spanish commission in England to ask for peace proposals, for to no power was American encroachment in the Pacific more annoying than to England."

The Associated Press denied the story the day previous in London.[53] On the following day the *New York Times* declared that it "put no faith whatever in the report" from the *Kreuz Zeitung*. On February 14, it was asked in the House of Commons if Great Britain ever proposed the note in question. Viscount Cranborne, under secretary of state for foreign affairs, replied, "No, Great Britain never proposed, through Her Majesty's ambassadors, or otherwise, any declaration adverse to the United States in regard to their intervention in Cuba. On the contrary, Her

Majesty's Government declined to assent to any such proposal." [54]

The actual story of events would seem to be simple. On April 14, 1898, through the efforts of the Spanish ambassador, a meeting was called in the office of Lord Pauncefote. The Powers had previously agreed that as doyen the British ambassador should be asked to draft a note of intervention. They felt that the Spanish note of April 10 might alter the situation. Sir Julian drafted the note, feeling that he might be able to make it more moderate than it might otherwise be. After the preliminary note had been read, M. Cambon, the French ambassador, took the note and revised it, changing the spirit of the note but scarcely altering the wording. Lord Pauncefote failed to see what had been done and signed the note as his own. Copies of the Cambon note were sent to the different foreign offices. When Dr. von Holleben cabled the note to Berlin he added these words: "Personally, I regard this demonstration somewhat coldly." The Emperor appended the following marginal note to the copy: "I regard it as completely futile and purposeless and, therefore, prejudicial. I am against this step." This note was said to have remained in the foreign office until in 1902 when it was used to refute the British protestations of friendship for the United States. Naturally the event grieved Lord Pauncefote greatly, particularly since the British Government, in its own statement, had not exonerated him. Some time later George Smalley, a newspaper correspondent, and a friend of Lord Pauncefote, secured the real story. This was cabled to the *Times,* together with a statement from President Roosevelt: "Not only do I not believe this Berlin story, but I know it is false." Lord Pauncefote died a few weeks later. It would seem safe to say that the "Holleben story" is false, and that Lord Pauncefote, through his failure to see the spirit of the Cambon note, had opened the way for this malicious report. At any rate, its effect had been simply to give added strength to the Anglo-American friendship.[55]

On April 9, General Fitzhugh Lee left Havana placing the American consulate in charge of the British consul-general. On the same day representatives of the six great Powers of Europe called upon the Spanish minister of state at Madrid and recommended a cessation of hostilities in Cuba. As a result, General Blanco was instructed to proclaim a truce, the length of which would depend upon his discretion.[56] Two days later President McKinley, wearied of Spanish evasion and suspicion, sent his war message to Congress.[57] While the members of the British government praised the moderate character of the note they regretted that President McKinley had turned affairs over to Congress, feeling that in so doing he had renounced his

[55] *New York Times,* February 6, 7, 13, 1902; *London Times,* February 6, 7, 8, 14, 1902; *St. James Budget,* February 13, 14, 21, 1902; Smalley, George W., *Anglo-American Memories,* second series (London, 1912), pp. 170-188.

[56] *Hansard's Parliamentary Debates,* Vol. LVI, p. 418; *London Times,* April 11, 1898.

[57] Richardson, *Messages and Papers of the President.* Vol. X, pp. 139-157.

future right of initiation and surrendered power to Congress.[58]   They regretted too that although Spain had delayed so long, Mr. McKinley had been unable to give the Sagasta ministry time to carry out their last promises.[59]   On the other hand, "The wonder to most of us," said Justin McCarthy, "was, not that the United States should have intervened at last, but that she had not intervened long before . . . . if America cared nothing as a State for the pleading of mere humanity, she would have to consider whether her own interests as a State did not compel her to the work of intervention." [60]   Generally, however, the British press praised the moderation of the note and felt that it had not brought war particularly nearer.[61]

Perhaps the most suggestive indication of Great Britain's attitude toward the United States during the interval of April 4 and 11 when the entire world felt that war was inevitable [62] is to be found in the *Saturday Review* which was always hostile to American interests. "When we find the bulk of the English newspapers calling on us to admire the attitude of the United States and accord our moral support to the Washington Government, it is time to protest." [63]

In general, Great Britain interpreted the causes of the war in a manner highly favourable to the Americans.   While her own interests may have influenced,

[58] *London Times,* April 11-14, 1898.

[59] *Ibid.,* April 12, 1898.

[60] McCarthy, Justin, "What England Feels," *The American-Spanish War—A History by the War Leaders* (Norwich, 1899), p. 492.

[61] *British Weekly,* April 14, 1898.

[62] *Pall Mall Gazette,* April 14, 1898.

[63] *Saturday Review,* April 9, 1898.

and probably did influence, this decision, there is no more reason to doubt the integrity of her sympathy than to discredit the sincerity of America in entering the war.[64] Most of the British newspapers agreed that the war had been brought on by three causes: humanitarian, in which she placed primary significance, the need for the protection of American commercial interests in Cuba, and the safety of American citizens resident in Cuba.[65]

On April 15, the *Pall Mall Gazette,* less hostile to the United States by far than the *Saturday Review,* but never actively friendly, said, ". . . they [the American people] are by no means clear either for what they are going to fight, or to what use they will put the success which, sooner or later, is bound to attend their arms. They intend, of course, to bundle the Spaniards out of Cuba, neck and crop; but for what purpose? Mr. McKinley has told Congress that there is no Government in Cuba that the States ought to recognize; nevertheless it is more than probable that unless the States do not recognize the 'so-called Republic of Cuba' the insurgents will receive their deliverers as they have the Spaniards."

On April 21, Secretary Sherman cabled Mr. Woodford to turn the legation over to the British embassy and to leave for Paris immediately. On the same day

[64] Cf. Dunning, *The British Empire and the United States,* pp. 321-322.

[65] *London Times,* April 2, 4, 1898; *Spectator,* March 14, 1898; "The United States and Spain," *Quarterly Review,* Vol. CLXXXVIII (July, 1898), pp. 216-241; McCarthy, Justin, "What England Feels," *The American-Spanish War—A History by the War Leaders,* pp. 489-508.

the Consul-General at Barcelona was ordered to turn over all consular affairs to the British consuls and leave Spain at once.[66] At the same time a fund was placed subject to British call for the relief of American citizens resident in Spain.[67]

Throughout April Great Britain took the utmost precaution to observe a strict technical neutrality. The British consuls everywhere sent formal notices of neutrality in response to a general proclamation issued at London.[68] Neutral trade privileges were carefully maintained, consular negotiations were carried on with the utmost precaution, and international law was zealously respected. It is safe to say that although British sympathy was usually exhibited in all British ports for American interests, there were very few, if any, open violations of official neutrality. It was, indeed, this very precaution which enabled Great Britain to be of the service she was to American interests.

[66] *Foreign Relations,* 1898, p. 766.

[67] *Ibid.,* p. 768.

[68] For a complete text of the Proclamation see the *London Gazette,* April 26, 1898; *Foreign Relations,* 1898, pp. 842, 843, 844, 850-851, 865-871; *London Times,* April 27, 1898.

CHAPTER V

ANGLO-AMERICAN RELATIONS IN THE WEST

WAR with Spain became certain on April 19, 1898, when Congress passed a resolution authorizing and directing the President to intervene at once to stop the war in Cuba. The previous day Henry Cabot Lodge of Massachusetts had introduced a bill in the Senate which provided that money be appropriated for the payment of the Bering Sea award to Great Britain pursuant to the stipulations of the Convention of February 8, 1896. The bill of appropriation had been drawn up by John T. Morgan of Alabama of the Senate Committee of Foreign Relations.[1]

[1] This bill was of peculiar interest to Great Britain at this time, for the following reasons: the sum of $473,151.26 had been awarded Great Britain by the commissioners appointed pursuant to the stipulations of the convention of February 8, 1896, which provided for the settlement of the claims presented by Great Britain against the United States in virtue of the convention of February 28, 1892. (See *United States Statutes at Large,* Vol. XXXIX, 55th Congress, 2d session, p. 470.) The Bering Sea controversy had continued a constant source of irritation between the two powers after the latter date, and the United States had failed to make the necessary appropriation for the award granted. On April 18, 1898, Senator Lodge of the Committee on Foreign Relations proposed a bill for its payment. "I desire to say," he said, "on the question of the reference of the bill, that the message of the President of the United States communicating the report of the commissioners came to the Senate on the 14th of January, 1898. In the pressure of the great question which has been before the country the matter I suppose has been

A second event following immediately upon the introduction of the Lodge bill was highly pleasing to the British merchants. As early as 1896, Great Britain had begun to be concerned over the fact that neither the United States nor Spain had signed the Declaration of Paris. At no time before the outbreak of the war had either state indicated what action she would pursue either toward privateering or toward enemy goods in neutral ships, or neutral goods in enemy ships.[2] In the earlier days of April, 1898, the British press suggested that if Spanish privateers should intercept American wheat and cotton ships they might throw half of Europe into a passion of apprehension and annoyance.[3] On April 20, a semi-official report reached Great Britain that the United States would act under the Declaration. British comment was very favourable.[4] On April 26, President McKinley officially announced that the United States would dis-

---

lost sight of. . . . It is a debt of honor and good faith." During the brief discussion of the bill Senator Lodge gave assurance that every member of the Foreign Relations Committee desired its payment. Even Senator John T. Morgan of Alabama spoke in its behalf. This act meant, then, that the United States was not only going to meet a debt long overdue to Great Britain and thereby help close the long controversy, but that the two men on the Senate who had been most critical of Great Britain in the past three years had acted in her behalf. (*Congressional Record*, Vol. XXXI, part 4, 55th Congress, 2d session, p. 4004.) Final settlement was made on June 15, 1898. (*Foreign Relations*, 1898, pp. 371-373.) The *Times* of April 23, definitely intimated the significance placed by the British press on this act. *Cf. post*, p. 89.

[2] *Pall Mall Gazette*, April 16, 21, 1898: *Statist*, April 5.

[3] *British Weekly*, April 28, 1898.

[4] *British Weekly*, April 28, 1898; *Pall Mall Gazette*, April 21; *Statist*, April 23, 1898.

countenance privateering. This decision at once lifted the war, so far as the United States was concerned, to a high plane of international law, a standard maintained throughout to the satisfaction of the British and the advantage of the Americans.

Convinced of the reciprocal interests of the United States and Great Britain as shown through these two events, the *London Times* of April 21 openly expressed British sympathy for the United States in the war. "They [the United States] will probably make some mistakes, as we almost invariably do, but with them as with ourselves, mistakes will only increase the dogged tenacity of purpose which knows how to convert mistakes themselves into stepping stones to success. Whether the struggle be brief or protracted, there can be as little doubt of the result as there is of the direction in which lie the sympathy and the hope of the English people."

The *Pall Mall Gazette* openly criticized the action of the *London Times*. It had already expressed support for the United States.[5] "The *Times*," said the *Pall Mall Gazette*, "signifies its [the war] arrival by the tardy declaration that there can be no doubt in which direction British hopes and sympathies will lie. It was inevitable that the *Times* would say that in the end, though those who have not made a study of its ways might not have thought so from its querulous tone hitherto, depending now upon one hasty view of things, now on a diametrically opposite one. But it was inevitable because there *is* no doubt of the trend of sympathy among the mass of this country. Of course,

[5] *Pall Mall Gazette,* April 16, 20, 1898.

like *every* other Power, we shall observe a strict neutral attitude. . . . The Americans will fight in a cause that commands the sympathies of this nation, and they are our kinsmen. For these reasons, and because the time has come when it is possible to abolish the ancient grudge and stimulate in America those feelings which have long been alive in England, the *Times* is right in its estimate of our hopes and sympathies." [6]

Following these statements of American appreciation, particularly that of the *Times*, various rumours began to develop in Great Britain to the effect that British interest was turning from the United States to Spain.[7] On April 28, it was suggested in the morning papers that a majority of Parliament favoured Spain. Two methods were used by the *London Times* to counteract these reports. On April 23, President McKinley's answer to the *Times'* article of April 21 was published. "You can say that the whole of the United States responds" to the expression of British friendship. Five days later the *Times* stated the American attitude toward Great Britain in specific terms.

"The United States," it said, "was anxious for British friendship. The President and the Americans in general have an opinion of England above that of all other states. She desires to consider English interests wherever possible. Before the blockade of Havana was declared, instructions were sent to the commander of the fleet to facilitate in every way the departure of the British residents. She is anxious to facilitate dip-

[6] *Pall Mall Gazette,* April 21, 1898.

[7] *London Times,* April 29, 1898; *New York Times,* April 29, 1898.

lomatic relations. An agreement for the reference of
the North Atlantic fishery question and Canadian
trade and commerce is nearly ready for British acceptance. The payment of the Bering Sea award is declared. Mr. John Adam Kasson has been substituted
for John W. Foster on the Anglo-American Joint
High Commission to settle disputes between the United
States and Canada. Finally the President is not only
willing that his good will toward Great Britain should
be made known, but he desires that there may be some
way provided by means of which coöperation on a
large scale may be carried on between the United
States and Great Britain." [8]

During the same days that the rumours of British
friendship for Spain were being reported, suggestions
of possible continental interference were likewise ap-
pearing. On April 23, the *Statist* said that some
powers may have wanted to intervene, but they knew
that Great Britain would never consent. She is
friendly to the United States but she will be neutral.
A week later this same paper became even more specific. "When the war between China and Japan broke
out, the Powers did not intervene, largely because the
British Government refused to join. The action of the
Continental Powers is stopped in the West Indies just
as it was stopped in the Far East. . . . The Continental Powers will not risk a war with the whole
English-speaking people. But if we allow matters to
drift, if we lap ourselves in the hope that no difficulties will arise, if we put off taking thought for to-
morrow, we may suddenly wake up one morning to

find that the Continental Powers have addressed an ultimatum to the United States." This time, the British people, "must not be found napping." [9]

After the declaration of war on April 25, Anglo-American relations in the West centred around three activities: the coast patrol and the blockade of Cuba, the maintenance of neutrality, and the protection of American interests in Spanish territory by British consuls. Early in January, 1898, Secretary John D. Long of the Navy Department began to organize the navy in preparation for possible action in Cuba. He proposed two lines of defence for the West. Patrol squadrons would be formed whose purpose it should be to protect the coast towns from bombardment and insure the safety of American trade. In this way he hoped to calm the fears felt by some Americans that the Spaniards might send privateers or a blockading squadron to the American coast, immediately upon the outbreak of hostilities. Furthermore, he hoped by the same means to assure Continental merchants and financiers, particularly the British, that the American trade would not be disturbed or endangered. So effective was this plan that although both the New York and London exchanges showed frequent slight disturbances, trade not only remained excellent throughout the months of January, February, and March, but actually improved.[10] By the close of the first week of April, 1898, British shippers had become so generally reassured that the *Statist* suggested that al-

[9] *Statist*, April 30, 1898.

[10] *Bradstreet's*, February 26, March 5, 12, 1898; see also *Statist*, March 5, 1898.

though Spain might be victorious in the beginning of the war, and might even blockade a few American towns, thereby temporarily disturbing the immediate British supply of wheat and cotton, little damage would be done, either to American property or Anglo-American trade.[11]

On April 30, 1898, *Bradstreet's* reported the business hesitation incident to the outbreak of the war so little as to amount almost to indifference.[12]

Mr. Long's second plan of campaign was the establishment of an effective blockade of Cuba immediately upon the outbreak of actual hostilities. He hoped in this way to prevent the landing of Spanish reinforcements, either of troops or munitions. On April 21, Secretary Long instructed Admiral Sampson to blockade Cuba from Cardenas to Bahia Honda if he considered it advisable, and on the same day he [Secretary Long] notified the Boston and Norfolk navy yards that although war was not yet declared it might be declared at any moment and that the North Atlantic Squadron was blockading Cuba.[13]

[11] *Statist,* April 9, 1898; *Cf. ibid.,* March 12, 1898.

[12] It is impossible to say just how definitely the financial world knew of Secretary Long's plans. Many, if not most of his naval orders were secret and confidential, still it would seem that a general idea of naval preparation was allowed to permeate business circles thoroughly.

[13] The organization of the fleet in the West was as follows: Rear Admiral W. T. Sampson, was commander-in-chief; *Blockading Squadron,* Commodore J. C. Watson, commanding from May 6, 1896, to June 21, 1898; *First North Atlantic Squadron,* Commodore J. C. Watson, commanding from July 21, 1898, to June 27, 1898; Commodore J. A. Howell, commanding from July 1, 1898, to close of hostilities; *Second North Atlantic Squadron,* Commodore W. S. Schley, commanding after June 21, 1898, to the close of hostilities;

On April 28, Secretary Long received information
through a London agent that the Spanish fleet under
Admiral Pasqual Cervera was still coaling at the Cape
Verde islands.[14]   The following morning Mr. Long
learned through the same source that four cruisers
and three destroyers had just sailed west.[15]   As a result of these notices, Mr. Long dispatched Captain. C.
F. Goodrich in command of the U.S.S. *St. Louis* and
Captain C. S. Cotton in command of the U.S.S. *Harvard* to ascertain whether the Spanish fleet which had
just left the Cape Verde islands intended moving upon
the West Indian islands, and, if so, toward what
locality.[16]

On April 30, Mr. Long learned through the same
London agent that the steamer *Avery Hill* on arrival
at the Cape Verde islands reported the Spanish fleet
continuing westward at full speed.[17]   For the next
two weeks no definite information was received.   The
most rigid blockade of the West Indies was maintained,
and Admiral W. T. Sampson held his fleet ready for

Flying Squadron, Commodore W. S. Schley, commanding from the
beginning of the war to May 24, 1898, independently—from May 24
to June 21, under the orders of Admiral Sampson; *Naval Base,* Key
West, Florida, Commodore George C. Ramey, commanding May 7,
1898, to August 24, 1898.   At the beginning of the war Commodore
Howell was given command of the Northern Patrol Squadron whose
duty it was to protect the coast and the coastwise trade between the
capes of Delaware and Bar Harbor, Maine.   See *Annual Report of
the Navy Department,* 1898, pp. 37-41.

[14] *Annual Report of the Navy Department,* 1898, p. 359.   The same
material with similar pagination may always be found in *House
Documents,* Vol. XII, No. 3, 55th Congress, 3d session, p. 359.

[15] *Ibid.,* p. 360.

[16] *Ibid.,* pp. 360-364.

[17] *Ibid.,* p. 364.

immediate attack whenever he should receive notice from the Navy Department of the exact location of the Spanish fleet.

During this time the British policy of benevolent neutrality was tested to the limit as a few illustrations will show.   On April 27, notice was given the *Somers,* a torpedo boat, stationed at Falmouth, England, to leave at once.   The boat did not have sufficient crew for immediate sailing, and enlistment in a foreign port was illegal.   As a result, it remained interned in the British port throughout the period of the war.   It was not until December, 1898, that Great Britain sanctioned its return, and then only when the United States had given an assurance that, in the event of hostilities being resumed with Spain, no use would be made of it.[18]

A comparison of this act with another will illustrate Great Britain's policy of technical neutrality. A Spanish ship was docked at Cork, Ireland, for repairs.   On April 21, Mr. Arthur Balfour declared its detention in the event of war between Spain and the United States as contrary to the practices of war since its repairs were uncompleted.[19]   In either case the boat was of considerable immediate importance to the country owning it.   The British might easily, in the first instance, through careless or intentional negligence, have allowed the enlistment of a foreign crew.   It would have been almost impossible for Spain to secure evidence of British guilt.   In the latter instance a reasonable delay in rendering a decision would not

[18] *Foreign Relations,* 1898, pp. 1006-7.
[19] *Hansard's Parliamentary Debates,* Vol. LVI, p. 962.

have been unusual, but it would have inconvenienced Spain.

On May 1, the English "tramp" steamer, *Strathdee* of Glasgow, was stopped by an American patrol ship and boarded by the United States for the third time on her trip between Progreso, Mexico, to Sagua. The captain was very amiable over it and suggested that he would probably be stopped several times more.[20] Between the time when it was first assigned to blockade duty and May 10, the U.S.S. *Eagle* stopped and boarded the British brigantine *Harry Stewart* and the British steamer *Adula*. The *Adula*, at the time it was stopped, was carrying refugees from Cienfuegos to Kingston, Jamaica. The passengers seemed free and willing to give any information they knew concerning the blockading activities.[21]

Out of a total of ten British prizes captured by the North Atlantic Fleet, five were condemned, three were released, and the disposition of two is given as "unknown."[22] The capture of one, the *Restormel*, attracted considerable attention. In April the rumour appeared, both in England and in the United States, that a shipment of Cardiff coal, intended for Spanish

[20] *London Times*, May 5, 1898.

[21] *Annual Report of the Navy Department*, 1898, pp. 186-187, 350; Sampson, Rear-Admiral William T., "The Atlantic Fleet in the Spanish War," *Century Magazine*, Vol. LVII (April, 1898), pp. 886-912. In no case noted did the British vessels seem at all disposed to object to being stopped. They showed their papers willingly and accepted the request as an acknowledged measure sanctioned by international law. Furthermore, particularly those destined for Kingston, Jamaica, frequently carried Cuban refugees.

[22] *Annual Report of the Navy Department*, 1898, gives a total list of the prize, pp. 316-325.

use, had been made. On May 10, the Navy Department received information from London that a quantity of coal had been placed in English ships and sent somewhere along the north coast of Venezuela for the purpose of supplying the Spanish squadron.[23] On the morning of May 25, the U.S.S. *St. Paul* gave chase to a steamer which was attempting to enter the harbour of Santiago. She proved to be the British steamer *Restormel,* from Cardiff, Wales, with 2400 tons of coal, evidently for the Spanish fleet. She had been at San Juan, Porto Rico, thence had gone to Curaçao, where she had been informed that the Spanish fleet had left two days before her arrival. She was then "directed to proceed to Santiago." Her captain frankly stated that he had expected to be captured. Both he and the crew seemed pleased with their failure to reach the Spanish. The collier, according to the captain, was one of a group of three sent from the same company under similar instructions. If the report be true that there were less than one thousand tons of coal in the possession of Cervera, the capture of the *Restormel* was a serious loss for the Spaniards.[24] The following morning another collier was captured, probably a second of the group of three.[25]

Immediately following the declaration of war all American consulates and embassies were turned over

---

[23] *Ibid.,* p. 390. This information from London had probably come from the same London agent to whom reference has been made previously. Although his name cannot be ascertained, his information seems to be considered authoritative.

[24] *Ibid.,* pp. 410-411, 413; *Cf.* also *War Notes* No. 1, Office of Naval Intelligence, Information from Abroad, pp. 34-36.

[25] *Annual Report of the Navy Department,* 1898, p. 399.

to the resident British officials. The extent of the
services they performed can hardly be estimated. They
provided for the safety of the lives of American citizens and for the protection of their property and their
business interests. They served as mediators between
the American and Spanish officials providing for the
comfort and exchange of American prisoners and for
the facilitation of official communications. Wherever
possible, in a besieged city, they cared for the needy
natives, distributed food and clothing, and cared for
the sick.

Generally, the Spanish officials recognized the British consuls as neutral and coöperated with them willingly. In some cases they curtly refused every favour
that the British Government had been commissioned
to request for American citizens.[26] The Spanish
civilian population, unaccustomed to the exchange of
international courtesies, often looked upon the British
with little less hostility than upon the Americans. The
correspondent for the *London Times* reported that
the populace about Corunna believed that the British
were allies of the Americans and planned to share in
the spoils of war.[27] Rumours were constantly appear-
ing in Great Britain that certain consulates had been
attacked by Spanish mobs.[28]

A few illustrations will show the varied and painstaking work done by the British consuls in Cuba. The
blockade, necessary for the conquest of the Spanish

[26] Kelly, Edmond, "An American in Madrid during the War," *The
Century Magazine*, Vol. LVII (January, 1899), pp. 450-457.

[27] *London Times*, April 29, 1898.

[28] *Hansard's Parliamentary Debates*, Vol. LVII, pp. 188-189.

army on the island, brought even keener suffering on the Cubans than it did on the Spaniards. Food was not to be procured. Dogs died of starvation in the open streets; horses, weakened from lack of food, fell in their traces and were left to die at the roadside; men, women and children were freqently found dead on the paths leading to the market place whither they had gone early in the morning hoping to procure a few morsels of food. Not only the American Government but private charities as well were anxious to extend relief.

About the 10th of May two volunteers, correspondents for the *New York World,* Thrall and Jones, were landed near Mariel for the purpose of instructing the rebels to come to the coast to receive supplies. The men were captured the same day by a Spanish patrol and taken to Havana for trial. Their only hope for escape from death as spies was in the influence of the British consul, who might secure a suspension of the extreme penalty. The United States Government on the evening of May 15, sent the gunboat *Uncas* under a flag of truce into the harbour of Havana in an endeavour to make terms and save the lives of the two men. Through the efforts of the British consul-general, Alexander Gallan, an exchange was secured, and the two correspondents were released.[29]

A few weeks later than this Lord Pauncefote informed Secretary Day that he had just received a telegraphic report from acting Consul-General Jerome saying that many United States citizens in Cuba who were in danger of starvation had applied to him for

[29] *London Times,* May 16, 1898.

relief. He desired to know what he should do in the
matter. The State Department at once placed two
thousand dollars to the credit of the consul-general
together with the request that the United States be
kept informed as to the extent to which relief might
be required in the future. A few days later Lord
Pauncefote reported that a total of 107 American
families had applied for relief; 34 were given aid;
4 were refused; and the remaining 69 families were
still under consideration. On August 10, Secretary
Day asked that "an expression of the Department's
high appreciation of his continued efficient and conscientious execution of its request" be extended Mr.
Jerome.[30]

A third illustration will show a still different type
of consular service. The Home Mission Board of the
Southern Baptist Convention owned a considerable
amount of property in Havana and San Miguel. It
was in charge of Dr. Ed Beloit, a French citizen, who
died early in the summer. The Mission Board then
authorized Miss Joerg, a niece and an assistant of Dr.
Beloit, to assume control. At the same time it re-
quested the Department of State to notify the British
consul of the new appointment in order that he might
render such good offices as might be needful and proper.
Soon after this an attempt was made by a man named
Sanchez to extort money from the Joerg mission—in
connection with the will of the late Dr. Beloit. The
former American vice-consul at Havana was an execu-
tor under the will. Mr. Jerome, acting British consul,
served with the French consul to protect the rights of

[30] *Foreign Relations*, 1898, pp. 998-1000.

the French and American heirs.[31]   In September, Mr. Porter King, chairman of the Southern Baptist Convention, and Miss Joerg sent to the British consul through Secretary Day a vote of thanks expressing their appreciation of the kindness and courtesy that he had shown them.[32]

By far the most spectacular instance of consular service was rendered by Frederick W. Ramsden, British consul at Santiago.   After sinking the *Merrimac* in an effort to block the entrance to the harbour at Santiago, Lieutenant Richmond Pearson Hobson and his crew of seven men were captured by the Spanish and put into the old Morro prison.   The cells were badly lighted, unsanitary, and poorly furnished.   Within an hour after the arrival of the Americans, men began to bring in furniture from Santiago.   A table, a washstand, a pitcher, a basin, a cot with a double blanket, and several chairs—one of them a rocker—were given to Lieutenant Hobson.   A cot and a blanket were provided for each of the men.   These were gifts from Mr. Ramsden and were but the first of many acts of kindness and attention on his part.   Shortly after the arrival of the furniture, the Consul, himself, came in order to investigate the safety and comfort of the prisoners.   On June 6, a general bombardment began and Morro Castle was in direct line of the firing.   Fortunately none of the Americans were killed.   The following day Mr. Ramsden secured their transfer to Santiago.   From then on the Consul called at least every third day on both Lieutenant Hobson and his men.

[31] *Ibid.*, 1898, pp. 987-989.
[32] *Ibid.*, pp. 987-989.

He sent them fruit, coffee, sugar, crackers, bread, tobacco, and cards. He secured hospital attention for the sick and out-of-doors exercise for all. Later he negotiated an exchange for them. Throughout the entire time of their imprisonment, he constantly guarded their safety, health, and comfort.[33]

Soon after this the struggle at El Caney began. In spite of the heat and exhaustion from overwork Mr. Ramsden remained in the city, sparing himself no strain in caring for the sick and wounded. It cost him his life, for he contracted the fever and died on August 10, at his home in Kingston, Jamaica. The "good-Samaritan of Santiago" had given his life to the cause of the American people and suffering humanity. There is probably no greater example of sincere, unselfish, loyal service to duty and humanity to be found in the entire history of the war.

As a recognition of his service General Wood ordered, on August 12, that all flags be put at half-mast. This act was reported at once by Lord Pauncefote to Mr. Alvey A. Adee of the Department of State. On September 17, Mr. Adee forwarded a note of appreciation to the British Government for the services rendered by Mr. Ramsden. This was followed a few days later by a second note of appreciation of the gratification of the British Government for the respect shown Mr

[33] Hobson, Richmond Pearson, *The Sinking of the Merrimac* (New York, 1899), pp. 228-251. The same story appeared previously in *The Century Magazine,* Vol. LVII (December 1898), pp. 265-283, (January, 1899), pp. 427-450; (February, 1899), pp. 580-604; (March, 1899), pp. 752-779.

Ramsden, and a further eulogy of the consul himself.[34]

No study of Anglo-American relations in the West would be complete without a consideration of the attitude of the British colonies toward the United States. There has grown up a generally accepted idea that the colonials were not friendly toward the Americans. Not only is this notion false but it seems safe to say that the colonials usually maintained an attitude of ✓ benevolent neutrality. It is true that Great Britain held as the fundamental requisite in her new foreign policy the promotion of good will between herself and her colonies. No matter what her immediate foreign situation might be she could not afford to scrifice for American interest her colonial support measured in terms of men, money, and munitions, and her own immediate necessity.[35] But Great Britain in her original declaration of neutrality left its maintenance entirely in the control of her colonials within their own borders. Although there were various rumours of broken neutrality on their part, favourable to Spain, no situation was reported in which the United States saw fit to refer the matter to the British Government.

On July 17, Michael Davitt asked the House of Commons if attention had been directed to the reports

---

[34] *Foreign Relations,* 1898, pp. 380-381. After the close of the war Mr. R. U. Johnson of the *Century Magazine* suggested to Mr. Long that a suitable memorial be erected for Consul Ramsden. This was done, and a heavy bronze tablet was designed by Robert G. Skerrett of the Navy Department and cast in the Washington Navy Yards. It is now affixed to the house in Santiago where Mr. Ramsden lived. A replica was set at the Naval Academy at Annapolis.

[35] *Literary Digest,* March 12, 1898.

that war supplies had been provided at Jamaica for the Spanish and what steps had been taken in that colony to enforce neutrality. Lord Curzon replied that the American Department of State had made no such representation. Jamaica had been provided with a copy of the Declaration of Neutrality and might be expected to provide for its observance.[36]

As a matter of fact, the U.S.S. *Harvard* had been forced to stop at Kingston, Jamaica, for coal and water. Since it was impossible for Captain Cotton to take on board this ship in twenty-four hours, with the facilities available at Kingston, the amount of coal necessary to carry her to the nearest home port, Key West, he asked to be allowed to remain in port thirty-six hours. The request was granted, together with a second request for an extension of time. The *Harvard* was allowed seven hundred and fifty tons of coal, and all the fresh water needed. "There was an apparent disposition on the part of the British colonial authorities to render every assistance that the attitude of the British government as a neutral power would warrant." [37]

Lieutenant W. H. Allen, in describing his trip around Cape Horn with the *Oregon*, reported that, although strict neutrality was observed at the British Barbadoes, "The sympathy of the Barbadians was clearly with us, and we were constantly advised to go in and whip the Spaniards." [38]   Early in May, the

---

[36] *Hansard's Parliamentary Debates*, Vol. LX, p. 945.

[37] *Annual Report of the Navy Department*, 1898, pp. 406-407, Report of Captain C. S. Cotton of the U.S.S. *Harvard*.

[38] Allen, Lieutenant W. H., "The Voyage of the Oregon," *The American-Spanish War—A History by the War Leaders*, p. 175.

London Daily Mail collected a group of editorials from British colonial journals illustrating their attitude toward the United States and the Spanish-American War. Praise, support, and appreciation were expressed for the United States by nearly every important colonial paper not only in the West but in the East as well. The *Singapore Free Press* was quoted as saying "opinions may differ as to the manner and occasion of that interposition, but no doubt this will liberate Cuba from a dominion that has long become intolerable." The *Shanghai Mercury* said, "It is in the interest of peace that America will fight. It is in the interests of civilization, order and good government that President McKinley has decided, and very properly, to intervene. 'We cannot but reëcho the sentiment of the Yankee captain taken at Taku—"Blood is thicker than water" and hope for the triumph of Anglo-Saxon civilization.' " The *Kingston Press* suggested that "America is more than justified in intervening in Cuba. . . . In stepping in and saying, 'these crimes against humanity and civilization must cease,' America has the sympathy and support of the civilized world." The *Kingston News Letter* said, "the Republic [the United States] will have the sympathy and support of Great Britain and her colonies all the world over." The *Gazette* [Indian] said, "There is only one feeling among Britons in India, and that is that America's position is impregnable from the point of view of humanity." [39] In New South Wales one hundred men offered their services to the American consul.

[39] Cf. *Public Opinion*, May 5, 1898, for extracts from the *London Daily Mail* symposium entitled, "Anglo-Saxon's Solid."

The attitude of the Canadians is probably more difficult to evaluate than that of any of the other British colonies. There was some, perhaps considerable, anti-American comment. A Study of four Canadian newspapers for the first half of the year 1898 will reveal this. At the same time it will give proof of considerable Canadian friendship. The *Montreal Daily Witness* was always frankly friendly. The editorials following the battle of Manila and the battle of Santiago expressed satisfaction over the American victories. Nevertheless, on May 3, 1898, it said, "Nothing strikes the close observer here [Toronto] more forcibly just now than the almost unanimity of the people in their sympathy for Spain in the present struggle. . . . The redeeming feature of the situation is the hope of an Anglo-American Alliance one outcome of which would be the more kindly and respectful treatment of Canada by the United States politicians." [40] The *Toronto Globe* seemed equally friendly. On May 2, 1898, it denied that the French Canadians were in sympathy with Spain and asserted that the chief interest of all Canadians was the development of Canadian nationality. There are, it concluded, neither "English Canadians" nor "French Canadians." On May 6, it suggested that an Anglo-British "unity" would be the welcome development of Commodore Dewey's guns at Manila. A few comments from the *Globe* for July 5, are suggestive: "It's in the blood; Britannia and Columbia rule the waves; we rather think now that the United States is an Anglo-Saxon nation." In an-

[40] *Montreal Daily Witness,* May 3, 1898, see also May 2, 4, 6, 7; June 28, July 4, 5, 6, 1898.

other issue it said, "On the sea the Americans are real sons of old mother England." [41] The *Ottawa Citizen* was inclined to be sarcastic and critical of the United States, but it was not particularly friendly toward Spain. On July 1, after criticizing the *New York Sun* bitterly for its tardy professions of British friendship, it said, "It seems to us that the English papers are getting altogether too sloppy in their Anglo-American-Alliance admiration of the prowess of Uncle Sam's troops." On the whole the paper often failed to be guarded or careful in its discussions of Spanish-American affairs. It cannot, though, be said to have been very unfriendly toward the United States.[42] The *Montreal Gazette,* though friendly to the United States, was inclined to emphasize the importance of Canadian nationality. At times it maintained an attitude that was critical toward both the United States and Great Britain.[43] Generally, then, it may be said that anti-American comment came almost entirely from three sources: the French-Canadians, the Canadian-nationalists, and a few anti-Americans who failed to understand the importance to Canada of the new relation which was developing between the United States and Great Britain.

Early in the war a few Canadian merchants began to realize that Canada would benefit from an Anglo-American alliance during the war. Inevitably Anglo-American friendship would lead the American people, in proportion as they desired British friendship, to

---

[41] *Toronto Globe,* May 4; see also May 2, 5, 6, July 4, 5, 1898.

[42] *Ottawa Citizen,* May 1-8, July 1, 4, 5, 1898.

[43] *Montreal Gazette,* May 2, 4, 9, June 30, July 4, 5, 12, 1898.

seek a settlement of all those questions of trade and boundary lines which had been accumulating between Canada and the United States for years.[44] But at this point the Canadian nationalists caused difficulty. As nationalists they desired that all the negotiations be conducted by Canadians in behalf of Canadian interests. They were suspicious of both the British and the Americans, for they realized that the former would make concessions which the Canadians would not.[45]

Perhaps the chief factor leading to friendship between the United States and Canada was the growing maturity of the two nations. With such a development petty jealousies became a matter of the past. Canada ceased to be afraid of American aggression as the United States abandoned her attitude of national superiority. Gradually Canada recognized herself as a great democratic nation in harmony with the political principles of both Great Britain and the United States and opposed to the monarchial theories of the nations of Europe. Out of this grew the idea that in case of war between Great Britain and the continental nations, the United States, under the Monroe Doctrine, would support Canadian nationality.[46]

Only once during the entire war did Canada's proximity to the United States endanger her neutrality. Early in June the secret service bureau obtained possession of a letter written by Lieutenant Ramon Car-

[44] *Literary Digest*, April 9, 23, 1898.

[45] *Congressional Record*, Vol. XXXI, 55th Congress, 2d session, p. 2471; "The Anglo-American Joint High Commission," *North American Review*, Vol. CLXVIII (August, 1898), pp. 165-175; *London Times*, January 1, May 24, 1898.

[46] *Literary Digest*, March 12, 1898; *Public Opinion*, June 16, 1898.

ranza, a former Spanish naval attaché. The writer declared himself to be the organizer of Spain's spy system in this continent, and acknowledged the capture by the United States authorities of two of his best spies. The letter in itself was of little importance, but the United States, Canada, and Great Britain were equally disturbed over its publication.[47] This feeling was intensified by the fact that the former Spanish minister to Washington had taken up his residence in Toronto,[48] and that a number of Spanish speakers had appeared from time to time in the city. A few Canadians as a result openly expressed sympathy for Spain.[49] The majority of the Canadians, however, were entirely neutral and critical of the Spanish attempts to influence Canadian sympathy. In July sufficient proof had been obtained of Spanish activities to warrant British intervention, and a number of Spaniards fround guilty of violation of neutrality were asked to leave.[50]

Closely allied to British colonial sympathy in its importance to Anglo-American relations in the West were certain elements of British appreciation of American activities. Nothing could be more pleasing to the American people than British praise. When the raw

[47] *Hansard's Parliamentary Debates*, Vol. LVI, p. 1210.

[48] *Ibid.*, Vol. LIX, p. 47.

[49] *Montreal Gazette*, July 12, 1898.

[50] *Hansard's Parliamentary Debates*, Vol. LXIII, p. 437. This action was taken by the direction of Great Britain rather than Canada. "The authority for such action rests upon the power of the Crown in such a case to expel an alien from Canadian territory." See *Public Opinion*, June 6, 1898, for American comments on the letter.

American troops assembled at Tampa no one knew their deficiencies better than the American Government. Yet with the exception of a very few British papers, chief among them being the *Saturday Review,* the British press was united in its favourable comments. They spoke of the infantry as seasoned men who appeared throughout as a most thoroughly "workmanlike" body of soldiers. They did not have the smart appearance that one looked for in a British Tommy Atkins nor was there the strict discipline and deference from men to officers when off duty customary in Europe. But there was a morale and an individual efficiency which was superior even to that of British soldiers. Seventy-five per cent of them were expert marksmen.[51]

Later on, as time passed and American action in Cuba seemed slow and inefficient, the British comments continued to be favourable.[52] Spanish delay in attack signified Spanish defeat. Great Britain saw, even better than the majority of the American people, the true situation. Spain was defeated on the sea, although the army in Cuba was untouched. The Americans might expect to meet resistance from those natives both in Cuba and the Philippines who hoped to reap the political fruits of victory. Great Britain saw also that the

[51] *London Times,* May 23, 1898. *The Illustrated London News,* April 30, 1898, gave pictures of "Types of the United States Navy." The men represented were of a very high order. On the same day it gave a picture of an American man-of-war preparing for action. The men were again pictured as of high order; *Graphic* supplement, April 30, May 14, June 11, 1898, gave representations of American sailors and naval officers which were very complimentary to the United States.

[52] *Pall Mall Gazette,* May 21, 23, 27, 31, 1898.

only solution possible for the native insurrections would be the conquest and civilization of those peoples. The Americans did not realize this until the urgency of the situation forced them to assume this responsibility. Furthermore, Great Britain realized that these islands must be kept safe from European vultures, principally Germany, who would not only snatch the islands but American trade as well.[53] Strange as it may seem, the British public were generally very late in their receipt of American news. It was not until June 6, that they knew what was happening in Cuba, and then only two subjects were cleared up. Admiral Cervera with six vessels was in the harbour of Santiago, and Admiral Sampson was on the outside of the harbour maintaining a blockade. It was not until July 5, that the news of the battle of Santiago on July 3 was published. The chief result was that when information was published in Great Britain it was generally accurate.

In conclusion, the war in the West had led to the development of Anglo-American friendship in a number of respects. In the first place, the United States realized for the first time the importance of British friendship. The western Atlantic had definitely become an Anglo-American sea with the United States and Great Britain in joint control. Furthermore, a new harmony had developed between the British colonies and the United States, which was essential to the development of Anglo-American harmony. Finally, Great Britain had recognized the United States as a world power and as essential to the development of the great theory of Anglo-Saxon politics.

[53] *London Times*, June 3, July 9, 1898.

CHAPTER VI

ANGLO-AMERICAN RELATIONS IN THE EAST

ON January 3, 1898, Commodore Dewey assumed command of the Asiatic squadron then stationed in the harbour of Nagasaki, Japan. The records which were turned over to him by Acting Rear-Admiral F. B. McNair mentioned little of interest. There was slight indication in them of the approaching trouble that was soon to assume critical aspects in China. They spoke of an uneasy state of affairs in Korea, some anti-missionary riots in Japan, the seizure of Kiaochow bay by the Germans one month earlier, and a few minor international matters. There was no suggestion of trouble in the Philippines and ". . . in no manner was there any forecast given of the work in which the squadron would soon be so vitally interested." [1]

The Asiatic station, however, as Commodore Dewey saw it at that time, held a strategic significance. The United States was inevitably drifting into a war with Spain. In command of an efficient fleet in the Pacific, with a freedom to act in consequence of being so far distant from Washington, he could strike promptly and successfully at the Spanish forces in the Philippines.[2] In every respect Commodore Dewey was the

[1] Dewey, George, *Autobiography of George Dewey* (New York, 1913), pp. 174-175.

[2] *Ibid.*, p. 168.

man best fitted to assume command of the Asiatic squadron. Thoroughly trained in the old school of naval efficiency, he had, nevertheless, become a profound student of modern naval science and procedure and international law. In temperament, in ability, and in experience he was thoroughly prepared to meet European naval tactics and diplomatic strategy.

Commodore Dewey's first concern, immediately after his appointment in October, 1897, had been relative to ammunition. Inquiry soon revealed the fact that there was not even a peace allowance on hand. A further supply had been ordered, but no effort had been made to facilitate its shipment. Largely through the efforts of Mr. Theodore Roosevelt, who was then assistant secretary of the navy, Commodore Dewey was able to have nearly thirty-five tons, or about one-half the total supply, shipped from San Francisco just before his departure on December 7. The remainder, about thirty-seven tons, was shipped to Honolulu, where it was transferred to the *Baltimore* in March, 1898. It finally reached Hongkong only forty-eight hours before the American fleet was forced to leave that harbour. It was actually transferred to the various vessels of the squadron on the day of the declaration of war. Even with this consignment they went into action in Manila Bay with but sixty per cent of their full capacity. There was no reserve.[3]

Shortly after his arrival in Nagasaki, Commodore Dewey asked for an audience with the Emperor of Japan. This had long been the custom of each new

[3] *Ibid.*, pp. 171-172.

commander-in-chief of the Asiatic squadron, but it
had recently fallen into neglect. The diplomatic courtesy proved valuable, however, for it established pleas-
ant relations between Commodore Dewey and the
Japanese Government which were to hold throughout
the trying days of the blockade in the harbour of Manila.[4] On February 11, he sailed for Hongkong where
he was to remain until the outbreak of Spanish-
American hostilities.

When Commodore Dewey had accepted his appointment in October, 1897, a war with Spain had seemed
possible to many Americans, but there had seemed
little or no possibility of European complications.
Indeed, for the time being Europe appeared outwardly,
singularly peaceful. On September 18, 1897, the *Spectator,* in an article entitled "England's Isolation," illustrated this fact very well. It maintained that Great
Britain was the keeper of the peace in Europe for three
reasons. In the first place, there were two great alliances in Europe, neither one of which held a balance
of power, without British support. Since a combination of the two alliances was highly improbable and
since Great Britain refused to ally herself with either
one, war was quite impossible. In the second place,
England was really stronger than she felt herself to
be a short time previously, and finally there had been
a gradual awakening of European statesmen to the
fact that Great Britain was no one's enemy. England,
it concluded, had gained rapidly in the last eighteen or
twenty months. The next issue of the *Spectator* called
attention to "persistent reports" of American interven-

[4] *Ibid.,* pp. 177-178.

tion in Cuba, but it gave no indication of European complications.[5]

A few days later the *New York Times* reviewed the earlier article from the *Spectator*. England's security, said the *Times*, "depends upon her own course, and nothing but rash aggressiveness of which she shows no indication in this generation can bring about any formidable hostile combination. This is the situation which the Americans can regard with satisfaction for whatever may from time to time be our differences with our elder brothers, we cannot be blind to the fact that they and we are the joint representatives and guardians of a principle of government that no other nation even fully understands—the principle of orderly freedom which is the hope of the race." The *Times*, too, saw no indication of approaching trouble.

In November, two German missionaries were murdered in China. China promptly offered immediate and full redress, but Germany seized upon the incident as a pretext for securing possession of Kiaochow.[6] Russia and France, alert to the situation, likewise demanded concessions. Europe at once faced the horrors of a world war. Quickly two policies of action assumed shape: Great Britain's theory of the "open door" and American penetration of Eastern trade and politics.

During the first days of January, 1898, the British

[5] *Spectator,* September 25, 1897.

[6] *London Times,* January 4, 1898; consult *Accounts and Papers,* 1898, Vol. LIV (*State Papers,* Vol. CV), for "Correspondence respecting the Affairs in China."

press announced the fundamental principles of the new British policy in China. "Our real interest in China is trade. . . . What therefore concerns us is that the Chinese markets should not be closed against us. . . . We do not for a moment suppose that either Russia or France or Germany will attempt to shut us out from these markets; and, provided they do not, it is no affair of ours to drive Russia out of Port Arthur, or Germany out of Kiaochow. Whether we ought to take possession of any portion of the Chinese territory requires serious consideration. If China is divided it may be necessary that we have certain parts under our control or other coaling stations than Hongkong. What would suit best our purposes would be a reform of the existing Chinese government and the throwing open of the whole empire to the world's trade. If this cannot be done without European seizure of Chinese ports, then the government must necessarily consider what our interests require. But nothing should be done hastily or out of mere jealousy of continental powers." [7]

Early in January, China appealed to Great Britain for a loan of sixteen million pounds sterling in order to pay off what remained of the indemnity due to Japan and secure the relief of Weihaiwei. With this loan as a basis for its discussion, the *Statist* carried the arguments which it had previously developed to

[7] *Statist,* January 1, 1898; the *Economist* made no attempt to develop a definite trade policy on that date. It did advise, however, popular support for Lord Salisbury's "policy of waiting." England's strength, it said, lay in the most powerful fleet in the Far East and in the fact that she controls every coaling station on the way to China; *Cf. Manchester Guardian,* January 3, 1898.

their logical conclusion. The result was the press draft of the British policy of the "open door." "Unquestionably," said the *Statist*, "we have no interest in getting Japan out of China. In the first place, when the war was over, one of the objects to which Japan applied herself was the opening up of China to all countries. Therefore, any influence that Japan may be able to exercise in China will be for the benefit of trade and not against it. In the second place, we have no reason either to fear or dislike Japan, and have no object, consequently, in hurrying her out of Weihaiwei. Nor does China herself seem to have any sufficient interest in hastening the withdrawal of Japan. If Germany is to retain Kiaochow, and Russia is to remain at Port Arthur, and France is to get some compensation, does it make any real difference to China whether or no Japanese troops remain in Weihaiwei for a few years longer." Finally, what we do want is a "free field and no favour." We want our trade to be unhampered, that we may have free competition for all concessions, and that there "may be no objectionable monopolies." If the Germans and Russians choose to hold concessions, that is none of our business. But it is our business to see that no prohibitive tariffs are imposed, and we ought to make it clearly understood to the Continental Powers that so long as they confine themselves to land grabbing we do not mean to offer material resistance, but that we will not tolerate pilfering from China if the pilfering is to be used to the detriment of our trade. As regards the Chinese Government we owe it no consideration. We should make it clearly understood at Pekin that if monopolies and unfair advantages are given to our rivals, we shall visit upon the Chinese Government the consequences of her own partiality. It may be necessary that we have additional coaling stations in the Far East and one or two ports in which we can refit vessels. If there is need, there is no reason why we should not help ourselves if Russia, Germany, and France set the example. "On the other hand, if [they] are willing to keep hands off, we [the European powers] might maintain the *status quo* as long as China will hold together." [8]

On January 10, 1898, Mr. Arthur Balfour, in a speech at Manchester, outlined the proposed policy of the Government in China. Our interests are commercial and trading interests, not territorial. Great Britain owns eighty per cent of the combined trade of the world with China. All we intend to do is to insist that "the policy of that government shall not be directed toward the discouragement of foreign trade." We do not want great accessions of territory carved out of the Chinese Empire. We are not opposed to the extension of commerce of any other nation in China, but England must be allowed to go there as well. Foreigners shall not destroy the equality of opportunity for trade for all in China.[9]

Hardly had the "open door" policy been generally

[8] *Statist,* January 8, 1898. This article gives probably the first and best complete outline of the new British "open door" policy in China. It makes no allusion to American interests in China or for the need of Anglo-American coöperation in the Far East; *Cf. Graphic,* January 8, 1898.

[9] *Economist,* January 15, 1898; *London Times,* January 5, 11, 1898; *Chronicle,* January 15, 1898.

announced when arguments began to be advanced to the effect that "spheres of influence" in China were incompatible with the treaty of Tientsin of 1858.[10] On February 8, Lord Salisbury, in an address before the House of Lords, answered these arguments and developed the final step in the "open door" policy. "We have not surrendered one iota of our Treaty rights. We have no intention of surrendering one iota of our Treaty rights . . . and there is no effort that this country will not make rather than allow those rights to be over-ridden." [11] Lord Salisbury then concluded that nobody [meaning any European statesman] has ever suggested the slightest intention of infringing any of the rights we enjoy under the treaty. Both the Russian and the German governments have given full assurance that any ports received by them would be made free ports.[12]

The weakness of the British "open door" policy as it was outlined in the early weeks of 1898, was this. It was based solely upon the guarantee of Russia and Germany. Both nations had voluntarily announced

[10] *Statist,* January 21, 1898.

[11] Under the treaty of Tientsin three articles were of peculiar interest. Article 24, Great Britain shall pay the same duties but none higher than are imposed upon other foreign states. Article 52, British ships of war with no hostile purpose shall be at liberty to enter all Chinese treaty ports and receive every facility for obtaining provisions and water. Article 54, the British government and its subjects will be allowed free and equal participation in the privileges, immunities, and advantages that may have been, or may be hereafter, granted by the Emperor of China to the government or subjects of any other nation.

[12] *Hansard's Parliamentary Debates,* Vol. LV, pp. 38-39; *Accounts and Papers,* Vol. LIV (*State Papers,* Vol. CV), 1898, Nos. 84, 151; see also *Statist,* March 5, 9, 12, 1898; *Chronicle,* February 12, 1898.

that British rights in the ports which they held in
China would be respected, and that those ports would
be open equally to the trade of all nations.   Great
Britain could only be sure of the maintenance of the
policy in proportion as she was willing to back it up
with force.   She recognized this weakness and proposed to secure the support of both Japan and the
United States.   Such an alliance she felt would be
of sufficient importance to prevent any violation of
the guarantee.

Fortunately for British purposes, conditions were
operating in the United States which served to make
Anglo-American coöperation in the East desirable.
Business had been prosperous for about two years.
The total output of manufactured goods was increasing rapidly.   American traders were searching for new
markets at the same time that China was being opened
up to European exploitation.[13]   A few Americans, particularly those who were interested in commerce and
finance, began to think in terms of British diplomacy.
They recognized, first of all, the similarity of Anglo-
American relations in Asia, but they did not appreciate the inability of Great Britain to protect those
interests without allies.   In the latter respect they
were in harmony with the criticisms advanced against
the British coalition government, not only by the Opposition but by many of the members of the party
in power.   On December 27, 1897, the *New York Times*
suggested, "We do not like Lord Salisbury's timid and
inactive policy in the East.   We in the United States

[13] *Chronicle,* January 1, May 9, June 11, 25, 1898; *American Review
of Reviews,* Vol. XVII (January, 1898), p. 13.

shall be the worse for it. Our interest in the cutting
up of China is that the British lion shall get his share."

On January 3, the *Manchester Guardian* presented
an excellent outline of the British policy in China.
The article, which was very acceptable to American
exporters, was quoted freely in American papers.[14]
A few American traders promptly recognized the importance of this opportunity and began to urge support for the British policy in the "open door."
Throughout January the *New York Evening Post* ran
a series of letters by Mr. Charles Denby, jr., and Mr.
Clarence Cary, urging the importance of American interests in China. In the partition of China, said the
Post, the United States has an interest, as our trade
there is second only to that of England. The present
Chinese tariff treats all alike, and China is the only
great field where the American manufacturer meets all
rivals on equal terms. The United States cannot tolerate the creation of spheres of influence since with the
seizure of territory our treaties with China which provide that American goods shall not be discriminated
against, and that no monopoly shall be granted to any
one, fall to the ground.[15] A few days later the *Review
of Reviews* again urged the necessity of the maintenance of American treaty rights in China. Our treaty
ports in China must be kept open to us on the present
terms. England has said plainly that she will not
allow the Continental Powers to seize China for pur-

[14] *New York Times,* January 4, 1898; *New York Evening Post,*
January 3, 5, 1898.

[15] *New York Evening Post,* January 1, 3, 5, 8, 1898; *Outlook,*
January 1, 1898.

poses of trade monopoly; and we must heartily join
England in this righteous position.

The *New York Times* urged American support for
the British "open door" policy from the first.   Early
in January it said, "England has acted with deliberation, but very much to the purpose in the matter of
German and Russian expansion in China.   It is clearly
a great injustice to represent England as engaged in
a game of grab.   She does not want more territory,
she wants more trade.   This trade is as free to traders
and ships of other nationalities, as the trade of other
treaty ports in which she is upon the same footing
with other powers." [16]

About a month later it advocated governmental
action.   The measure of our interests is the growth to
us during indefinite future time of the right of export
and import trade with the Chinese people.   "The
United States Government should employ serious measures for the protection of this trade.   It may be that
the United States has neglected English recognition
already too long." [17]   A few weeks later the *Times*
took occasion to say that our own Government should
express its sympathy with the British position.   In-
stead of doing this, the administration merely gave
out an announcement that our interests were not
threatened by the German and Russian proceedings.
It is to be hoped that the American government will
immediately appreciate the laxity of its action and
will come immediately to the English point of view.

[16] *New York Times,* January 4, 1898. *Cf. ibid.,* January 9, 1898;
New York World, January 4, 1898.
[17] *New York Times,* February 7, 1898.

We left England to make her fight alone, and if she has made it for her own exclusive benefit we cannot complain.[18] Four days later the *Times* announced the condition of Anglo-American relations as it saw them. The London dispatches are entirely credible which assure us that the sympathy of England is with us in respect to Cuba and also that England would be very glad of our support in the contest that she is carrying on single-handed, Japan excepted, in the Far East. England was bound to sympathize with us in Cuba. The British press understands the evils to trade of the chronic condition of war in Cuba, and she refrains from imputing to us motives of aggrandizement and conquest. We are fighting England's battles in Cuba, as England is fighting our battles in the East.[19]

On January 7, the *Tribune* stated that "the trade of China must remain open on equal terms to all the Powers," declares Great Britain. "The question for American consideration is whether or not this country

[18] *Ibid.*, March 6, 1898.

[19] *New York Times,* March 10, 1898. No better illustration can be found of the intense interest of the American commercial world in the British "open door" policy than is to be obtained from a consideration of the reception given to Lord Charles Beresford by the American Chambers of Commerce when he was in the United States early in 1899. Lord Beresford was then returning to England on his way from China where he had gone to investigate trade conditions for the British associated chambers of commerce. He addressed the San Francisco Chamber of Commerce. In Chicago business on the Board of Trade ceased entirely for the moment when he was introduced—an event absolutely without precedent. At Washington he was greeted both by President McKinley and John Hay. Letters of regret were sent him by a number of American trade organizations because of his inability to address them. See— Beresford, Lord Charles, *The Break-up of China* (New York, 1899), especially pages 433-446.

is to join them [European Powers] to secure Chinese trade. . . . Of all the great Western Powers, it lies nearest to China. . . . It is by nature and by situation fitted to enjoy the major share of all Pacific commerce. It rests with it now, without delay, whether it shall improve or shall forfeit its matchless opportunity." A few days later, January 10, the same paper commented, "of all the European Powers Great Britain is the one that stands for equal rights in international dealing. For any other to gain control of China would mean exclusion of all rivals from Chinese trade, or at least such handicaps as would practically amount to that. But wherever the British flag is raised there is freedom. When Great Britain secures the opening of another Chinese port or the free navigation of a river it is not for herself alone, but for all comers on equal terms."

Naturally the British sought to crystallize this growing American policy of intervention in China into a definite alliance with Great Britain in the East. On January 1, 1898, the *Statist* in its first appeal for the "open door" declared that "the United States has precisely the same interest in China" as Great Britain.[20] Early in the year Li Hung Chang had issued an appeal to the United States for support. "Should China be distressed by having her shores invaded and her territory occupied because of an occurrence which Western countries would deal with by law? Our desire is to preserve our territory intact and steadily improve it as a field open to all countries equally for the development of commerce." This appeal was distinctly

[20] *Statist,* January 1, 1898; see also *Statist,* May 5, 1898.

pleasing to the *London Times* for it placed American interest in China on a humanitarian basis. Such a call would move the American people more easily and quickly than a call for new markets. On January 5, the *London Times* published a brief symposium of American opinion quoting from three New York dailies, the *Times,* the *Herald* and the *World.* Quoting from the *Times* it said that Great Britain is not the champion of British interests alone; she is the champion of civilization and humanity, and deserves the support of all mankind, especially of the United States, for American interests in the East are the same as hers. According to the *Herald,* Americans know well where American interests lie. Germany, Russia, and France will set up a monopoly, each for its own behoof; but England will set up free trade, admitting American products as freely as English. The comment from the *World* was even more suggestive. The protest of Great Britain will stop the proposed spoliation of China and be indorsed by the conscience of the civilized world. The best of American opinion is with England and England knows it in spite of the jingo press. The Executive and Senate are in accord on the Chinese question. "A vigorous query will be put by the United States to any European Power occupying any one of our twenty or more treaty ports." [21]

Upon his arrival at Hongkong on February 17, 1898, Commodore Dewey must have begun to view the situation in the East with a new vision. The exploita-

[21] The last sentence quoted from the *World* was attributed to Cushman K. Davis, Chairman of the Senate Committee on Foreign Relations.

tion of Chinese trade seemed inevitable unless Great
Britain was able to require Germany and Russia to
keep their promises to grant an "open door" to trade
in all Chinese ports which were occupied by them.
American manufacturing interests had expressed
strong approval of the British policy. The British
were urgent in their appeal for American coöperation
in the Far East. Events fraught with startling import occurred in rapid succession.

On March 8, Prince Henry of Prussia, brother of the
German Kaiser, arrived at Hongkong with the rank
of rear admiral. The event was significant in that
it indicated that Germany was prepared to maintain
her interests in the Far East. To interpret his being
sent there as an act hostile to the United States is at
once illogical and inaccurate. Should an European
war ensue, German interests as well as British depended upon American friendship. The British would
need active American coöperation and Germany would
desire American neutrality. Any hostility shown by
Germany toward the United States would accomplish
only what it was to Germany's interest to prevent,
namely: to draw Great Britain and the United States
into commercial accord in China.

By the beginning of April, it had become clear to
Commodore Dewey that in case of war with Spain
the position of the American squadron in the East
would be very critical. Once hostilities had actually
begun, there would be no place close at hand where
supplies of coal could be procured or repairs made on
any vessels. He had made every effort possible before
he had left the United States to insure a prompt ship-

ment of munitions. Now he proposed to buy coal in the East and with a full supply of coal and munitions to avoid the necessity of having to seek shelter in any neutral harbour. In other words, he planned to be so well prepared and equipped for action that he would defeat the Spaniards in his first engagement.

On April 4, he cabled Secretary Long of the Navy Department that he had chartered the British steamer *Nanshan,* which had over 3,000 tons of coal on board. At the same time he advised the purchase of the vessel before the outbreak of hostilities.[22] Two days later the Government not only approved his action but advised him to buy that ship and one more. The crews in charge were to be enlisted, if possible, for a period of one year unless sooner discharged.[23] On April 6, the *Nanshan* was bought and her crew enlisted. On April 9, the British steamer *Zafero,* with supplies, was purchased in addition. The crew of this ship also was retained.[24]

Between March 8 and April 25, the date on which the American squadron left Hongkong, a number of events occurred to test Admiral Dewey's knowledge of diplomacy and international law. Shortly after the arrival of Prince Henry, a sailor believed to be a deserter from the American navy was located on the German cruiser *Gesion.* The American demand for his surrender was met by the assertion that he was a German subject and a seaman in the German navy,

---

[22] *Annual Report of the Navy Department,* 1898, p. 66; Dewey, *Autobiography,* p. 188.

[23] *Annual Report of the Navy Department,* 1898, p. 66.

[24] *Ibid.,* p. 66. *Cf.* Barrett, John, *Admiral George Dewey* (New York, 1899), p. 57.

and in neither capacity could he be given up.[25]   Some time later Prince Henry gave a dinner on board the *Deutschland,* his flagship, at which representatives of Great Britain, Russia, and the United States were guests of honour.   In the toasts the President of the United States was relegated to the last place.   The absence of the American officers from a few entertainments given in the Prince's honour soon brought a sincere apology from the Prince in person.   His plea was that his lack of experience was responsible for the slight.[26]   Considerable reliance may well be placed upon his apology.   The Prince was young, impetuous, and inclined to act according to his own fancy rather than according to naval etiquette.   Commodore Dewey's reply to the indiscretion indicated his knowledge of social naval procedure and his determination to have the respect due his country.

Throughout this period of naval inactivity Germany was very much concerned over America's intentions both in Cuba and in the East.   She was in no way pleased to see the United States acquire territory in either sphere.   During one of the frequent conversations in which Commodore Dewey and Prince Henry engaged, the latter remarked that he did not believe that the Powers would permit the United States to acquire Cuba.   Commodore Dewey replied that the Americans did not desire to annex Cuba but that they could not permit existing conditions to continue there at our very doors.   Some time later the Prince jokingly asked concerning the "general scramble" for

[25] Dewey, *Autobiography,* p. 182.
[26] *Ibid.,* pp. 182-184.

ι foothold in the Far East, "and what are you after? What does your country want?" To this Commodore Dewey responded, "Oh, we need only a bay." [27] The answer was evasive and insinuated just enough about the German seizure of Kiaochow to worry Germany. Unfortunately it was just such statements as this that served to stimulate German activities in Manila. Her interests were highly involved in the East. She felt that she must know what was to be done with every foot of territory. Weak Spain was a most satisfactory neighbour in the Philippines; Great Britain or the United States would not be so.

During the delay at Hongkong the sympathy and good will of the British naval and army men were constantly with the Americans. American officers and men were welcome guests at all British clubs and social gatherings. A spirit of camaraderie gradually developed between the two services that was highly indicative of the feeling that was developing between the two nations. There was, however, a strong tendency among the British to exaggerate the difficulties and dangers of an isolated attack upon the Spaniards at Manila. In the Hongkong club it was not possible to get bets, even at heavy odds, that the American expedition would be a success. Commodore Dewey was told, after a dinner at which his officers had been entertained by a British regiment, that the general comment among the British was, "A fine set of fellows, but unhappily we shall never see them again." [28]

[27] Dewey, *Autobiography,* pp. 184-185.
[28] *Ibid.,* p. 192; *Cf.* Barrett, *Admiral George Dewey,* p. 63; *London Times,* March 28, 1898.

On April, Commodore Dewey sailed out of Hongkong. As the American ships passed the vessels of the British fleet, the bulwarks of the latter were thronged with eager soldiers and sailors. The latter might not cheer, but the convalescent soldiers of the hospital-hulk were able to express British feeling by a hearty round of applause.[29]

The British press followed Admiral Dewey very closely after he left Hongkong. It rightly judged that he had orders "to see that the Spaniard squadron does not leave the Asiatic coast," and then conduct "offensive operations in the Philippine Islands." [30] It admitted little question of the issue of such a battle.[31] On May 1, the *New York Times* gave a careful review of the attitude of the British press towards the United States. "Of all the English newspapers of London only two, and they are minor ones, in any way suggest any pro-Spanish feeling. These are the *Morning* [32] and the *St. James Gazette*. Among those who stand firm for American friendship is the old Tory,

[29] Calkins, Lieutenant C. G., "The Naval Battle of Manila," *The American-Spanish War—A History by the War Leaders* (Norwich, 1899), pp. 103-128; Lieutenant Calkins gives one interesting rumour concerning the entering of Manila Harbour. The Americans were accused of having a British pilot and a gunner who had been recruited at Hongkong and that they were aided in getting into the harbour by a British steamer that led the way. The rumour is without foundation. It was later reported and denied in the House of Commons on July 19, 1898. *Hansard's Parliamentary Debates,* Vol. LXII, p. 297.

[30] Dewey, *Autobiography,* p. 195; *Annual Report of the Navy Department,* 1898, p. 65.

[31] *London Times,* April 26, 1898.

[32] The *Morning* as *Morning Herald,* was incorporated with the *Daily Express* in 1899.

the *Globe.* The *Westminster Gazette* suggests freely that if anything should happen England would suffer immense grief. Going straight through, the English press stand unanimous in favor of the United States." The *Times* failed to mention that the *Saturday Review* was exceedingly bitter toward the United States.

On May 1, Commodore Dewey defeated the Spanish squadron in the harbour of Manila. In the afternoon Consul O. F. Williams was sent on board a British ship with instructions to request her captain to be the bearer of a message to the Spanish captain-general. The message was finally delivered by the British consul, Mr. E. H. Rawson-Walker. It contained the general plan for further American action in the harbour. If another shot was fired at the American ships from the Manila batteries, the American ships should destroy the city. If there were any torpedo-boats in the Pasig River, they must be surrendered. If the Americans were allowed to transmit messages by the cable to Hongkong, the captain-general would also be permitted to use it. So carefully did these instructions cover the situation, and so faithfully was the Spanish promise of their maintenance kept that Admiral Dewey actually acquired a safe base seven thousand miles from home.[33]

---

[33] The Spanish captain-general refused Dewey's request for a joint use of the cable. On the next morning Admiral Dewey ordered the *Zafero* to cut the cable, and both the Spaniards and Americans were cut off from all communications with the rest of the world. Dewey, *Autobiography,* pp. 223-225; Barrett, *Admiral Dewey,* p. 86; *Annual Report of the Navy Department,* 1898, p. 68; *Hansard's Parliamentary Debates,* Vol. LVII, p. 268. The writer has recently been informed through reliable sources that one line was actually left uncut

On May 2, news of the battle of Manila began to
filter into Europe through Spanish sources. It was
generally admitted that Spain was defeated. Secretary Alger declared that it was a glorious victory but
refused to make any further comment. Both Secretary Long and Assistant Secretary Roosevelt refused
to talk.[34]

Vague rumours continued to come in throughout
May 3. London was the real centre of American news.
Secretary John Hay became the centre of questions and
congratulations. Even the Parnell members of Parliament sent a note of congratulation to President Mc-
Kinley.[35] British naval officers were unanimous in
sympathy and congratulations. On May 4, no news
came. The suggestion began to be made that the
Philippines might be turned over to Great Britain.[36]
On May 5 and 6, no news arrived, but no fear was
felt for Commodore Dewey. On May 7, certain circles
in Great Britain began to be anxious. Some gloomy

and messages came into the United States Naval Department regu-
larly by way of London and New York. The *Pall Mall Gazette*,
May 3, 1898, reported a rumour both from Paris and Madrid to the
effect that the Americans had cut the cable at Manila and taken the
end of it on board the cruiser *Olympia* for the purpose of establishing
communications with the United States.

[34] *New York Times,* May 2, 1898; *Pall Mall Gazette,* May 2, 1898.

[35] The note read as follows: "In the names of millions of Irishmen
the Parnellite Members of the House of Commons send you their
congratulations on the most brilliant victory of the American fleet."
It was signed by John Redmond. This is quoted from *London Times,*
May 2, 1898.

[36] *New York Times,* May 4, 1898. On May 3, the *New York Times*
reported that on the Saturday previous a speaker in the Cortes had
suggested that the Philippines might be used as security on which
to invoke the intervention of some European Power.

onjectures were made.[37]   On May 8, definite infor-
nation finally came and Great Britain and the United
States were both elated.[38]

Colonel George A. Loud, who went on board the
McCulloch when it was sent to Hongkong to carry
news of the victory, said that it was most pleasing to
see the gratification of the English people at Hongkong over the American victory. It seemed that the
Americans at home could not be more delighted. "As
they [the British] put it: Blood is thicker than
water." [39]   The British at Hongkong throughout Commodore Dewey's occupation of Manila never lost this
uniform interest and cordiality. Indeed, they were so
liberal in their interpretation of the laws of neutral-
ty that he had to be especially careful to commit
no act that might be misconstrued.[40]

The relation of the American fleet to foreign vessels
in Manila Bay was of necessity covered by international law. In general, it might be expected that the
leading naval nations of Europe would send vessels
there with the purpose of securing naval educational
information together with a small naval squadron relative in size to the importance of their commercial
interests and the number of their citizens in the
islands.[41]   In every case these vessels were supposed to

[37] *London Times,* May 7, 1898.

[38] *New York Times,* May 2-8, 1898; *New York Herald,* May 2-8,
1898; *London Times,* May 2-8, 1898; *Literary Digest,* May 14, 1898.
Cf. speech by Lord Salisbury—reported in *London Times*, May 9,
1898.

[39] Loud, Colonel George A., "The Battle of Manila," *Century
Magazine,* Vol. LVI (September, 1898), p. 618.

[40] Dewey, *Autobiography,* pp. 240-241.

[41] *Hansard's Parliamentary Debates,* Vol. LVII, pp. 42, 176.

apply to Commodore Dewey for anchorage space, to report all movements in or out of the harbour, and to carry on no intercourse either with the insurgents or the Spanish land forces.

Immediately after the battle of Manila foreign men-of-war began to arrive. The British ships *Linnet* and *Immortalité* came on May 2 and May 7 respectively. The German cruisers *Irene* and *Cormoran* arrived on May 6 and 9.

Quickly international complications arose. The American flagship *Olympia* was off Cavite; the American colours were flying over the Cavite naval station and the authority of the United States was clearly paramount in the bay. In view of these facts, the British, French, and Japanese steamers as they came in reported to Commodore Dewey and secured proper anchorage. The *Irene,* sailing from Nagasaki, may not have known of the victory before leaving Japan, but she did receive definite information from a British steamer on the morning of her arrival. Nevertheless she steamed past the *Olympia* and dropped anchor where she chose. Commodore Dewey overlooked this first instance of the violation of the law of blockade.[42]

The second German cruiser, the *Cormoran,* came in at three o'clock in the morning. A steam launch was sent out at once to meet her and identify her. The *Cormoran* paid no attention to the launch. As a result the *Raleigh* fired a shot across her bows. She stopped immediately. The boarding officer assured the Captain of the *Cormoran* that the Americans had no thought of being discourteous and had no desire to

[42] Dewey, *Autobiography,* pp. 254-255.

raise any ill feeling. Their only desire was to fulfill the laws of blockade and to protect the American ships against any Spanish ruse that might be attempted.[43]

The reasons for these violations of neutrality would seem to be clear. Germany was insistent upon knowing what the United States proposed to do in the harbour. If the Philippines were to be opened to exploitation, she proposed to have her share of the spoils since the geographical location of the islands was such that the nation or nations that secured control of them acquired considerable influence in the Far East. The situation was unique and critical. Germany proposed to place herself in a position to secure Spanish favour and to demand concessions equivalent to those received by her rivals in China. Her attitude toward the United States is less easily stated. Until the battle of Manila the German press had been, in the main, openly hostile to the United States. The officers of the Government, however, repeatedly gave semi-official assurances of German neutrality both through statements to the press and to diplomatic officials.[44]

On May 12, Vice-Admiral Otto von Diedrichs arrived in his flagship, the *Kaiserin Augusta*. This made the third German cruiser in the Bay. On May 6, the *Darmstadt*, a transport, had arrived with fourteen hundred men for relief crews. Commodore Dewey gave permission for the transfer, which should have been

[43] *Ibid.*, pp. 255-256.

[44] White, Andrew Dickson, *Autobiography* (New York, 1905), Vol. II, pp. 144, 160-161, 170, 177; *Literary Digest,* April 30, May 7, 1898; *Public Opinion,* May 5, 1898; *New York Times,* May 1, 7, 8, 1898.

accomplished promptly. The *Darmstadt,* however,
with her force of men nearly equal to the total number
of Dewey's crew, remained at anchor for four weeks.[45]

Since Vice-Admiral von Diedrichs' rank was superior
to that of Dewey's, it was necessary that the latter
make the first call. This he did, and, in the course
of the conversation, he referred to the presence of
the large German force and to the limited extent of
German commercial interests. This really amounted
to a polite inquiry as to the intentions of the German government. Admiral von Diedrichs' only answer
was: "I am here by order of the Kaiser, sir."

On May 20, Secretary Long notified Admiral Dewey
that reports were current to the effect that some
Spanish transports with a large body of troops were
sailing to the Philippines. Nine days earlier the *London Times* had stated that the American attaché at the
London embassy had cabled his Government that four
cruisers and three torpedo boats belonging to the Cape
Verde Fleet had arrived at Cadiz on May 10.[46] This
meant that, in all probability, the Americans would
be required to fight a second naval battle for which no
adequate preparation could be made. Troops, ships
and munitions were all needed. On May 27, Secretary
Long cabled that the *Monterey* was being sent to the
Asiatic station. Three days later the *Monadnock* was
likewise ordered to the East.[47]

[45] Dewey, *Autobiography,* p. 57.

[46] On May 12, Commodore Dewey reported to Secretary Long that
this fleet had left the Cape Verde Islands April 29. Its present where-
abouts was unknown. This report was not officially confirmed until
June 18. See *Annual Report of Navy Department,* 1898, p. 97.

[47] *Ibid.,* pp. 101-102.

On May 29, Secretary Long gave Admiral Dewey temporary relief by reporting that the Spanish force was not then en route to the Philippines. This meant that the *Charleston* and transports of troops under Brigadier-General Anderson might arrive in time to assist in the battle which might be necessary.[48]

Throughout the latter days of May, Anglo-American cordiality in the East continued to develop. On May 17, the *New York Tribune* suggested that the American fetish of isolation must be cast down, that the United States could no longer be a political hermit. Even Western newspapers began to see the desirability of an Anglo-American coöperation. They saw need for an "open door" for the American merchant marine, and the need of a navy to protect the great American carrying trade that should once more be revived.[49] At the same time Great Britain was becoming more definite in her opposition to any European conquest of the Philippines. On May 25, the *New York Times* quoted directly from the *London Times* of the day previous. "We could not look with indifference upon the acquisition of the Philippines by either France, Russia, or Germany"; though we have enough on our own hands not to care to add to our responsibilities in that quarter unless we should be compelled to do so "in order to prevent the islands from being used to obstruct the development of open trade. . . . We could contemplate their possession, however, by the United States with equanimity, and, indeed with satisfaction. We can only say that while

[48] *Ibid.,* p. 101.
[49] *Public Opinion,* May 18, 1898.

we would welcome the Americans in the Philippines
as kinsfolks and allies, united with us in the Far East
by the most powerful bonds of common interest, we
should regard very differently the acquisition of the
Archipelago by any other power."

Unfortunately during the weeks of May and June
when the relations between the British and the Americans had been growing more cordial, the attitude of
Germany toward the United States had been growing more and more open to question.   Rumours of
German hostility toward the American invasion of the
Philippines began to appear simultaneously with the
arrival of Admiral von Diedrichs in Manila on May
12.   On May 11, it was reported in London that Germany was actively preparing to signify her disapproval
of an American occupation of the Philippines, and
that this plan was acceptable to Austria.   The German consul at Manila was said to have received definite
instructions concerning Admiral Dewey.[50]   On May
12, it was reported in London that Germany had demanded an interest in the Philippines and might demand exclusive control of Samoa as her price of acquiescence to American control in the Philippines.
On the same day it was reported that three great
powers were determined to prevent America from
bringing war into Europe and that German intervention alone prevented the bombardment of Manila by
Commodore Dewey.[51]

About this time the German press seemed to change
its tone.   Actually it did not.   The important jour-

[50] *New York Times,* May 12, 1898; *London Times,* May 11, 1898.
[51] *New York Times,* May 13, 15, 1898.

aals, under Government orders probably, began openly
o favour the American cause.[52] The less important
papers still printed vast pages of news, most of it
not true, and most of it in favour of Spain. On
May 15, the *London Times* reported the German
Kaiser as saying "the Emperor may be trusted not
to suffer the friendship of a hundred years with the
State in which millions of Germans have found a
second home to be disturbed without serious reasons."
At the same time rumour continued to associate the
Philippines and Great Britain together. They were
to be offered to the British to cement the Anglo-Saxon
alliance.[53] The British in turn would give the Americans a trading post. Much of this confusion came
of necessity from the fact that the greater proportion
of the American people were not ready, as yet, to
embrace an imperial policy of commercial and colonial
expansion. Had the United States openly asserted
after the capture of Manila its intention of remaining in the Philippines, there is much reason to believe
that the Germans would never have entered the Bay
with military intent.

Within a week after Dewey's victory at Manila an
official of the German foreign office called at the American embassy in Berlin and formally inquired whether
the Americans intended to remain in the Philippines or
whether they would withdraw. Andrew D. White hap-
pened to be out of the office at the time; so Mr. John

[52] White, Andrew Dickson, *Autobiography* (New York, 1905), Vol.
II, pp. 160-161, 168; *Literary Digest,* April 30, May 7, 1898; *Public
Opinion,* May 5, 1898; *New York Times,* May 1, 1898.

[53] *New York Times,* May 15, 16, 1898.

Brinkerhoff Jackson, first secretary of the legation, gave
the reply. He was unable, he said, to say anything on
the subject, as he had no means of knowing the intentions of the American Government. The answer
might have been quite different had Mr. White
been present. Mr. Jackson's own opinion was that
the Germans wished to take advantage of the
slightest opportunity to land a force and thus
pave the way to a kind of protectorate over the
Philippines.[54]

The whole situation actually amounted to this: Germany wanted a foothold in the Philippines. Had
Spain been victorious in the battle of Manila, the
islands would have remained in the hands of a weak
state, much to the satisfaction of Germany. With
the United States victorious the situation became complicated. Obviously a large proportion of the American people would not consent to a permanent occupation of the islands. This would mean that the islands
must either be returned to Spain or transferred to
some European power. In the latter case Germany
was determined that she must have such recognition
as would balance her strength in the East with that
of Great Britain.[55]

During the first week of June the repeated assertions
of the German Government in favour of American
friendship began to influence American opinion. Gradually the rumour began to appear that the United

[54] The writer is indebted to Lieutenant-Commander Edward Breck,
Assistant Naval Attaché in Berlin during the Spanish-American war,
for this information.
[55] *New York Tribune,* June 6, 1898.

States had nothing to fear from Germany. It was reported upon the authority of Andrew D. White that Germany was not hostile to the United States. On June 5, 1898, the *New York Tribune* reported a prominent American as saying that there had been a complete change of public opinion in Germany. The German official telegraph agency published a dispatch to the effect that the German warships had gone to Manila for the sole purpose of protecting subjects of the German Empire. This was quoted freely in the United States.[56] On the same date the *New York Times* reported that the *Frankfurter Zeitung* and the *Cologne Gazette* had become friendly to the United States.

At the same time Germany's real motives began to appear more definitely. She wanted a share in the spoils. On June 13, it was reported from Singapore that the German Consul at Manila had been in prolonged conferences with the Spanish authorities. This had led to the belief that Germany had designs on the Sulu Archipelago. Prince Henry of Prussia, at Kiaochow, was kept constantly informed as to the developments in the war. During these same days, June 14 and 15, dispatches from Madrid urged German intervention and assistance.[57] On June 17, the *Berlin Marine Politische Correspondenz* was reported as saying, "For the same reasons which justified us in demanding the cession of a harbor from China we must claim one from the 'Republic of the Philippines' which to all appearances will be the issue of the present

[56] *New York Times*, June 4, 5, 7, 17, 1898.
[57] *New York Tribune*, June 14, 15, 1898.

affairs." [58]   On June 27, the *New York Times* called
attention to the fact that the Kaiser felt that the
Americans were exhibiting a tendency to depart from
their policy of seclusion and to interfere in the affairs
of the Old World. The German and Spanish fleets,
the Kaiser continued, would be more than a match
for any fleet America could produce which would not
tax the Union in ships and sailors. "It is not certain
that Germany has not a motive for such an alliance,
for the United States with Monroeism is nearly as
much in the way of Powers desiring to expand as
Great Britain." [55]

This, then, was the situation in Manila at the
end of the month. Admiral Dewey had received no
supplies either of munitions, ships, or men. There
were five German men-of-war in the harbour, two
of them having a greater displacement than any of
the American ships. Admiral Camara, who was in
command of the Cadiz reserve squadron, might appear
in Manila at any time. He had with him two powerful armoured cruisers the total displacement of which
was 18,200 tons, while the displacement of Dewey's
squadron was but 19,098 tons.[60]   Besides this, the
Spanish vessels carried two 12.6-inch and four 11-inch
guns while Dewey's largest calibred guns were but 8-
inch. The relief crews brought in on the *Darmstradt*
had not yet been transferred.

It was during the days of June 26-July 1, that the

[58] *London Times,* June 17, 1898.

[59] *New York Times,* June 27, 1898; *Spectator,* June 18, 1898.

[60] Dewey, *Autobiography,* p. 259; *Annual Report of the Navy Department,* 1898, p. 108.

American situation was most critical. On June 26,
Admiral Dewey cabled Secretary Long that the British
consul had informed him that he had orders to telegraph in cipher to his Government all movements of
the German men-of-war in the Philippines.[61] On June
27, Admiral Dewey suggested to Secretary Long that
should the coast of Spain be threatened the fleet under
Admiral Camara would have to return. Two days later
Secretary Long cabled Admiral Dewey that a squadron
under Commodore J. C. Watson was being prepared
with all possible dispatch for operations on the
Spanish coast. "The Spaniards know this." [62]   On
June 29, the report was given out that an American
fleet under Rear Admiral Watson had sailed for
Spain.[63] The next day General Anderson arrived at
the Philippines with the first land troops as reënforce-
ments for Admiral Dewey.

On June 30, the *New York Times* suggested that the
presence of the British warships at Manila would
destroy the probability of any undesirable dispropor-
tionate and unbalanced display of naval strength there
by any other power.[64] On July 1, the same paper
called attention to the fact that, in view of the German military display in the Philippines, England
might think it desirable to bring her squadron to the

[61] *Cipher Messages,* Vol. II, "Communications in the Office of Naval
Operations," p. 253.

[62] *Annual Report of the Navy Department,* 1898, p. 109.

[63] This fleet was actually never sent abroad. See *Annual Report of
the Navy Department,* 1898, pp. 37, 38, 109. See also *New York
Tribune,* July 22, 1898.

[64] There was a British fleet of three ships under Sir Edward Chichester in the harbour.

same force as Germany. If so, America would not feel obliged to object.

Late in June, the *New York Post* reported that an agreement had been arrived at between the German Ambassador and the American Secretary of State concerning the mission of Admiral von Diedrichs. The German press was greatly aroused. On July 1, the *Cologne Gazette* stated that, "Admiral von Diedrichs requires no instructions from Washington as to what he is to do or leave undone. So long as he does not interfere so as to obstruct or to promote the enterprise of the two belligerents, neither Admiral Dewey nor Secretary of State Sherman [sic] is competent to give him any directions whatever." On the same day the *Berliner Lokalanzeiger* asserted that, "A German Admiral knows quite well in what fashion he has to maintain the interest of his countrymen. He would most energetically repel any impertinent attempt to meddle in his affairs. This is the proper answer to the presumptuous Yankee." [65] The results of these statements seem obvious.

At this time the British formed the opinion that the Germans were determined to secure a footing in the Philippines.[66] This meant that although Great Britain would maintain a technical neutrality she would lend all support possible to Admiral Dewey at Manila. This opinion is well illustrated in the attitude of the British toward Admiral Camara at Port Said. As usual the imperial government depended upon the colonial officials to enforce the neutrality

[65] *Cf. London Times,* July 2, 1898.
[66] *Hansard's Parliamentary Debates,* Vol. LX, p. 800.

laws. First the Egyptian government prohibited the sale of coal to the Spanish vessels other than a sufficient amount to carry them back to Spain, and, at the same time, limited their stay in the port to twenty-four hours. After this Camara attempted to buy coal in spite of orders. This was again refused. Next he tried to re-coal from his own colliers, enlisting Egyptian stokers. Then he was ordered to leave at once. As he passed through the canal, he stopped at Suez, but was again warned off.[67] In this way Egyptian neutrality prevented Spanish action.

Throughout the latter part of June and the early part of July, Admiral Dewey was forced to use the utmost diligence in order to enforce the laws of neutrality upon the German Admiral. German officers frequently landed at Manila and were on cordial terms with the Spaniards. Indeed, the rumour was current in the city that the Germans would intervene in behalf of the Spaniards.[68]

On July 5, Admiral Dewey on board the *McCulloch* sailed around the German ships in an effort to convey the idea that he was not pleased with their proceedings. On the 6th he was informed that the German cruiser *Irene* was interfering with the operations of the insurgents against the Spaniards in Subig Bay. This was contrary both to international law and to Dewey's wishes. On July 7, Dewey sent the *Raleigh* and *Concord* to Subig to inquire into the truth of this report.

[67] Dewey, *Autobiography*, p. 260. *Cf. London Times*, July 1, 1898.
[68] *Cf.* Dewey, *Autobiography*, p. 262; Kraft, Herman F., and Norris, Walter B., *Sea Power in American History* (New York, 1920), pp. 318-320.

When they steamed into the harbour, the *Irene* promptly steamed out.[69]   Later Prince Henry attempted to explain this incident.   The *Irene,* so he said, had gone to Subig Bay to take off some Spanish women and children.[70]

The British frankly accepted the opinion held by the Americans concerning the *Irene* incident; that is, that Admiral von Diedrichs had disregarded comity, if not law, and that his act was one which the German Government ought either formally to approve or to disapprove.[71]

After the first of July with the information concerning Admiral Sampson's victory at Santiago and Camara's return at hand, Admiral Dewey was free to state his position concerning the laws of blockade to Admiral von Diedrichs.   This he did in a most positive manner.   The German Admiral denied Admiral Dewey's contentions but agreed to submit the point to a conference of all the senior officers of the men-of-war in the harbour.   At this meeting, only Captain Chichester of the *Immortalité* appeared.   He not only sustained Admiral Dewey's interpretations, but informed von Diedrichs that the British Government had ordered its

[69] *Annual Report of the Navy Department,* 1898, p. 110; Dewey, *Autobiography,* p. 264; Barrett, *Admiral George Dewey,* p. 115.

[70] *New York Times,* July 28, 1898.   *Cf.* Stickney, Joseph L., *Life of Dewey* (Chicago, 1898), pp. 287-288; *New York Tribune,* July 7, August 3, 1898.

[71] *London Times,* July 15, 16, 1898.   Later Baron von Bülow, Minister of Foreign Affairs, said that Germany had never been disloyal to neutrality in the East and that the newspaper reports of alleged German designs or German support of the Filipinos against Americans were the most barefaced falsehoods.   *London Times,* July 25, 1898.

ships to comply with even greater restrictions.[72] The British had now for the first time openly and positively asserted their support of the Americans.

Admiral von Diedrichs was still unwilling to accept Admiral Dewey's regulations. Presently the *Cormoran* appeared in the Bay. Determined that she should report, in keeping with the custom of other men-of war, Admiral Dewey sent the *McCulloch* under Flag-Lieutenant F. Brumley to meet her. The *Cormoran* then turned and steamed toward the northern part of the Bay, compelling the *McCulloch* to follow her. Lieutenant Brumley, after first giving a signal for communication, fired a shot across the bows of the *Cormoran*.

The following day Admiral von Diedrichs sent an officer to Dewey with a list of grievances. Admiral Dewey then took occasion to give the officer a firm and positive statement of his attitude toward the actions of the Germans in the Bay. Admiral von Diedrichs went immediately to Captain Chichester for advice. His reply was "that only Admiral Dewey and himself knew what would happen if the situation came to the worst." [73]

Throughout the latter part of July and the first of August events drew rapidly to a close in the Philippines. On July 17, the second expedition of land forces under Brigadier-General Francis V. Greene

[72] Dewey, *Autobiography*, p. 266. *Cf.* Stickney, *Life of Dewey*, pp. 87-93.

[73] Palmer, Frederick, *George Dewey, Admiral*, p. 17. The writer has been informed by Mr. Palmer that he secured this information from conversations with Admiral Dewey and with Flag-Lieutenant Brumley.

entered Manila.[74] On July 25, the third expedition of
troops under Major-General Wesley Merritt arrived,[75]
and six days later Brigadier-General Arthur McArthur
followed with the fourth division. On August 4, the
Monterey and the *Brutus* at last sailed into Manila.
Under the cover of darkness the first of the German
vessels sailed out of the harbour that night.

Admiral von Diedrichs made one more attempt to influence the British. Since reinforcements had arrived, it became necessary for the Americans to occupy the city. Admiral Dewey tried, without success,
to secure the unconditional surrender of the Spaniards.
A bombardment thus became necessary. Admiral
von Diedrichs, in an effort to spare the city, sent
word to Captain Chichester that he was coming on
board the British ship in order to induce him to
join in a protest against Dewey's proposed action.

Captain Chichester looked up international law and
spread a number of books out on his cabin table with
the pages opened and marked. When the German
Admiral arrived Sir Edward simply suggested: "What
can I do? This American admiral is so deadly right
in all that he has done and all that he proposes to
do, that, if we protest, we will surely show that we
do not understand the law. Of course there was nothing to be done and I did it." [76]

On August 9, the foreign men-of-war were notified
to move out of range. The British moved to the south-
ward on the American side; the Germans drew to the

[74] *Annual Report of the Navy Department,* 1898, p. 117.
[75] *Ibid.,* p. 118.
[76] Kraft and Norris, *Sea Power in American History,* p. 319.

northward, opposite the city, where they were still in the range of high shells. On August 13, the battle occurred. As the American vessels sailed for action the officers and men of the *Immortalité* crowded on her deck. Her guard was paraded, and her band played a favourite number of Admiral Dewey's, "Under the Double Eagle." As the American vessels came into action, Captain Chichester, with the two ships *Immortalité* and *Iphigenia,* moved into position between the American and German ships.[77] The British had spoken with a decision that left no question. The city surrendered without German interference.

The next morning the foreign men-of-war were officially notified that the city had been taken and the port was open. Captain Chichester alone of all the foreign officers acknowledged the notification by firing the national salute of twenty-one guns with the American ensign at the main.[78]

In summary, the attitude of Great Britain in the East during the Spanish-American war was as follows: First of all, she had maintained a technical neutrality throughout. She had extended no favours to the Americans at Hongkong that were not sanctioned by international law. She had accepted and obeyed the blockade at Manila. She had furnished no supplies nor aid that were forbidden. She had assisted in the care and transportation of Spanish refugees. It was, however, a benevolent neutrality which left no question as to which belligerent she favoured. On May 25, Admiral Dewey cabled Secretary Long that the

[77] Dewey, *Autobiography,* p. 277.
[78] *Ibid.,* p. 280.

British both in Manila and Hongkong were most friendly.[79] British subjects sold both coal and ships when war was inevitable, and British seamen were enlisted as their crews under American service.[80] Great Britain provided most of the coal that Admiral Dewey was able to secure. In Egypt in the case of Camara she enforced a neutrality that worked to the advantage of America. At Hongkong, where no Spanish ships were at hand, she offered equal privileges to both nations. Her consuls at both Cairo and Hongkong were frankly friendly to American interests. At Manila her consul, E. H. Rawson-Walker, performed the trying duties of Acting United States Consul in a most able and painstaking manner. He was of "invaluable assistance" to Admiral Dewey, being his "only means of communicating with the Spanish authorities and the chief agent in the protection of foreign residents." [81] The British press with few exceptions was always favourable toward Admiral Dewey and American interests in the East. The members of her Government were openly friendly.

Considerable question has always been raised as to the extent of Captain Chichester's influence in Manila. In the first place, he and Admiral Dewey

[79] *Cipher Messages,* Vol. II, "Communications in the Office of Naval Operations," p. 189.

[80] *Annual Report of the Navy Department,* 1898, p. 66; Dewey, *Autobiography,* pp. 191-192. Admiral Dewey did not man and arm the *Zafiro* and the *Nashan* as directed by the Navy Department. He registered them with their English crews as American merchant steamers cleared for Guam.

[81] *Foreign Relations,* 1898, p. 375; Dewey, *Autobiography,* p. 234. Mr. Rawson-Walker's health was broken down during this period largely because of the added burdens. He died August 2, 1898.

were firm personal friends, spending much time together.[82]   On at least four different occasions during the blockade Chaptain Chichester rendered a positive decision in favour of the Americans.   While it may be true that the Americans by themselves might have been able to withstand German aggression in the Philippines, the position maintained by Captain Chichester convinced Admiral von Diedrichs that Great Britain would resist German aggression to the limit. In other words, Germany was not yet prepared to meet the British in a great conflict.   The union of the American and British nations held the balance of world power as Joseph Chamberlain had planned.

[82] Barrett, *Admiral George Dewey,* pp. 26, 70, 101, 113, 131.

CHAPTER VII

The Anglo-American Rapprochement— A Conclusion

Throughout January and February of 1898 there was a constant agitation in the United States and in Great Britain in favour of the promotion of Anglo-American friendship. In March, the first distinct rumours of the need for a definite alliance began to appear. On March 14, the *London Times* correspondent at Madrid reported the possibility of an Anglo-Japanese-American entente. About the same time it was reported that a majority of the members of the House of Commons were in favour of an alliance. During the first week in April, the rumour of an actual Anglo-American alliance reached New York and spread rapidly over the country.[1] The press of both countries accepted it seriously and, in the main, favourably.[2] It was the type of report most opportune as the background for Mr. Chamberlain's great speech at Birmingham on May 13.

[1] Callahan, James M., *Cuba and International Relations*, p. 490.

[2] *Literary Digest*, April 30, 1898; "An Anglo-American Alliance," an editorial, *Outlook*, Vol. LVIII (April, 1898), p. 1060-1062. On April 9, the *Spectator*, always very friendly to the United States, said, ". . . if America were really attacked by a great Continental coalition, England would be at her side in twenty-four hours." The comment attracted considerable attention both in the United States and in England and was quoted freely.

Throughout this period John Hay was directing American interests in Great Britain. On April 21, he responded to the toast of Mayor Davies at the Lord Mayor's banquet with the significant speech of the evening. After calling attention to the fact that for nearly three generations there had been constant peace with a growing friendship existing between the two countries he said: "The good understanding between us is based on something deeper than mere expediency. All who think cannot but see there is a sanction like that of religion which binds us in partnership in the serious work of the world. . . . We are joint ministers in the same sacred mission of freedom and progress, charged with duties we cannot evade by the imposition of irresistible hands." [3]

The speech was greatly appreciated by the British in that it expressed all that was highest in Anglo-Saxon idealism. Furthermore, it interpreted and stated Anglo-American relations in terms of peace and progress rather than of aggression and commercialism. An editorial in the *Century Magazine* expressed this reciprocal feeling well. Great Britain, in the present crisis, "appreciates the dignity of the position maintained by our government, and recognizes, to some extent at least, the fact that our people in general are dominated in this matter by sentiment and a sense of justice, and not by covetousness." [4] However, commercial and selfish may have been the motives of the few who urged an Anglo-Saxon agreement, by far the

---

[3] *New York Times,* April 21, 1898; John Hay, *Addresses of John Hay* (New York, 1907), pp. 77-80.

[4] *Century Magazine,* Vol. LVI (April, 1898), p. 152.

greater majority were influenced entirely by principles of sentiment and altruism.

Throughout the early part of the year the Opposition criticized the Coalition foreign policy severely. This criticism was directed, however, against British foreign inactivity rather than against the possibility of an Anglo-American alliance. Unfortunately, very few, even of the members of the party in power, realized the danger of Great Britain's "splendid isolation" and her absolute dependence upon a foreign alliance. Consequently, soon after the victory of Commodore Dewey at Manila, Joseph Chamberlain considered that the time had come to present the Coalition foreign policy openly to the British people. His reasons were these. In the first place, the importance of American trade interests in the East was constantly becoming better understood and appreciated in the United States. At the same time, due to the determination of the Opposition to force Lord Salisbury to adopt an active, aggressive policy in his relations with Germany and Russia, Great Britain's position in China was becoming very serious,[5] and her need for an ally was growing correspondingly imperative. Moreover, the Opposition, under the leadership of Sir William Harcourt, had seemed to assume leadership in the promotion of Anglo-American friendship. Finally, after having been advised by Mr. Hay not "to let the Opposition have a monopoly of expressions of good will to America," [6] Mr. Chamberlain decided to

[5] *New York Times*, April 3, 1898.

[6] Thayer, William Roscoe, *The Life and Letters of John Hay* (Boston and New York, 1908), Vol. II, p. 169.

take his own constituency at Birmingham into his confidence, and on Friday, May 13, he gave them a frank analysis of his own views.[7] He hoped thus to allay the growing British opposition to Lord Salisbury's policy of foreign inactivity and to assure the American people of the friendship of the Coalition government.

This speech was at once the most significant and the most strategic of Salisbury's third ministry. It revealed with unmistakable clarity both Great Britain's military weakness and her imperative need of an alliance. It was immediately subjected to a storm of criticism. Within a few days, however, Parliament rightly arrived at the decision that Mr. Chamberlain had spoken in complete harmony with the policy of Lord Salisbury,[8] and that the Government was committed to a policy of Anglo-American friendship which should break down Great Britain's isolation and give to the English speaking race again the balance of world power. In general, the British press interpreted the speech accurately. They admired its honesty and the virility of its challenge. They commented upon its Far Eastern policy according to their own political predilections. Almost without exception, however, they urged the wisdom of an Anglo-American alliance.[9]

On May 16, the *London Times* gave a frank sum-

[7] See *London Times*, May 14, 1898, for a complete text of the speech. See *ante* Chapter II, pp. 20-21, for an analysis of the speech.

[8] *Hansard's Parliamentary Debates*, Vol. LVII, pp. 1386-1519, *passim*.

[9] *London Times*, May 14, 15, 16, 17, 1898; *Pall Mall Gazette*, May 14, 17, 1898; *Spectator*, May 21, 28, 1898; *Literary Digest*, May 28, 1898; *Public Opinion*, May 19, 26, 1898.

mary of the foreign comment on the speech. Its absolute honesty and daring, so different from European
methods of diplomacy, astonished and confused Continental diplomats and critics. From Paris to Berlin
and from Vienna to Madrid, they were in a quiver over
the speech. The Germans were almost shocked by its
clear, vigorous, and unconventional language. Some
said that it was a "declaration of the bankruptcy not
only of the past English policy, but—what is more—
of the whole power of England." Others declared that
Mr. Chamberlain underestimated the power of Great
Britain, and that in so doing he had killed all possibility of an Anglo-American alliance. The United
States would not attack Russia to pull the chestnuts
out of the fire for England. Besides this, he had threatened Russia and had admitted the overthrowing of
the Anglo-Japanese policy of coöperation. The comments proved that Mr. Chamberlain was right in his
belief that the speech would not injure England in
Europe. Europe did not believe what he said. On
May 15, the *New York World* analyzed the effect of
the speech in London. Uneasiness was produced on the
stock exchange, war rumours were freely circulated,
grave international complications were predicted, and
precautionary insurances were reported to have been
effected at fifteen guineas per cent against the risk of
war between France and Great Britain within the next
six months. "The British heart throbs for" the United
States.

The French comments were equally suggestive. No
after-dinner speech had ever produced such an effect.
Certain papers held that it was an attack on France.

Others declared that an Anglo-American alliance would
be challenged by Europe at large, beginning with Germany and Russia; while still others were very much
concerned over the nature of the alliance that was to
be formed. It cannot be, they said, with either Germany or Russia.[10] Neither nation saw that Mr. Chamberlain was actually offering the United States naval
protection in Manila in return for American support
in China.[11]

The satisfaction with which the speech was received
in the United States was astonishing.[12] On May 14,
the *Chicago Tribune* said, "There may never be such
an alliance in formal written terms. And there may
be. But what is unmistakable, not only inevitable, in
the future but actual in the present, actual and potent,
is this: that the two great branches of the Anglo-Saxon race are drawing nearer and nearer together
for coöperation in peace, and, in logical sequence, in
war as well. Every word that promotes that movement is to be welcomed and applauded. Well to the

[10] *Literary Digest,* May 28, 1898; *Public Opinion,* May 19, 26,
1898; *London Times,* May 16, 1898; *Pall Mall Gazette,* May 14, 15,
16, 1898.

[11] Thayer, *Life and Letters of John Hay,* Vol. II, p. 165.

[12] The significant sentences in the speech as most Americans interpreted them read thus: Our next duty "is to establish and to
maintain bonds of permanent amity with our kinsmen across the
Atlantic. I do not know what arrangements may be possible with
us, but this I know and feel, that the closer, the more cordial, the
fuller, and the more definite these arrangements are, with the consent
of both peoples, the better it will be for both and for the world.
And I even go so far as to say that, terrible as war may be, even
war itself would be cheaply purchased if in a great and noble cause
the Stars and Stripes and the Union Jack should wave together over
an Anglo-Saxon alliance."

fore among such words are those spoken by Mr. Chamberlain, directly to an English audience, but indirectly and no less meaningly to all the world."

On the following day the *Tribune* expressed the opinion that while an Anglo-Saxon alliance was not "likely" the two nations "should live on terms of amity, so that if it is best at any time that they should act together there will be no existing bad feeling to make it more difficult for them to do so." The following day, May 16, the *Tribune's* comment was exceedingly suggestive. After noting that the speech had "aroused the wrath of the Dons," it continued: "It is evident that Spain looks at it [an Anglo-American alliance] as a possible avenue of escape from its present desperate situation and will seek to arouse the hostile prejudices of the powers by calling their attention to the menace to their interests involved in such an Anglo-Saxon combination in the hope that Europe may take Spain's part." [13]

On May 14, the *New York Times* quoted the speech freely but with little comment. On May 15, it said that the speech read more like a revelation than a forecast. If the President had power to draw up secret treaties, it would seem that there was an alliance in existence much stronger than a friendly understanding. Mr. Chamberlain "completed the most memorable speech that an English audience in either hemisphere had listened to in a generation. We as well as continental countries will certainly conclude that the understanding has reached a more definite stage than was believed." Whatever may be the possibility of an

[13] *Cf. New York Times*, May 16, 1898.

European combination, the *Times* continued, this will lessen it.[14]

In the Anglo-American comment that followed Mr. Chamberlain's address, certain factors became evident. Foremost among them was the assurance that neither the mass of the British nor American people were yet ready for an alliance as that word is generally understood in European diplomacy. Equally clear was the fact that the two great English speaking peoples understood each other as never before and that out of this understanding there might come a mutual recognition on the part of the leaders of both that was to be more effective and more lasting than any paper alliance of modern times. A consideration of public opinion in the two states during the next few weeks will show this conclusion to be correct.

Among those prominent Americans who sought to promote an Anglo-American friendship, if not an agreement, throughout the critical months of 1898, certain names stand out in prominent relief. First among them, of course, was John Hay, who more than anyone else represented in Great Britain the highest ideals of American citizenship and diplomacy. To him more than to any other American belongs the credit of creating and directing British support for the United States throughout the war. Closely associated with him in his immediate work were President McKinley and Secretary of State William R. Day. These two, together with Sir Julian Pauncefote, moulded

[14] *New York Times*, May 14, 15, 1898. *Cf. Literary Digest*, May 28, 1898; *Public Opinion*, May 19, 26, 1898; *Harper's Weekly*, May 28, 1898.

Anglo-American diplomatic relations and public opinion in the United States in much the same way as Lord Salisbury, Joseph Chamberlain, and John Hay did in Great Britain.

Following closely behind these three in personal influence came Richard Olney, former secretary of state. He can state his own position best. "There is a patriotism of race as well as of country—and the Anglo-American is as little likely to be indifferent to the one as to the other. Family quarrels there have been heretofore and doubtless will be again, and the two peoples, at the safe distance which the broad Atlantic interposes, take with each other liberties of speech which only the fondest and dearest relatives indulge in. Nevertheless that they would be found standing together against any alien foe by whom either was menaced with destruction or irreparable calamity, it is not permissible to doubt. Nothing less could be expected of the close community between them in origin, speech, thought, literature, institutions, ideals, in the kind and degree of civilization enjoyed by both." [15]

Agitation in favour of an Anglo-American alliance, as has been intimated already, came in a number of well-defined movements. Throughout the winter and spring of 1898, many individuals and most journals

[15] Olney, Richard, "International Isolation of the United States," *Atlantic Monthly,* Vol. LXXXI (May, 1898), pp. 577-588. This was considered one of the most significant articles of the month. It was quoted freely both in Great Britain and in the United States. Bryce, James, "The Essential Unity of Britain and America," *Atlantic Monthly* (July, 1898), p. 28, gives a British consideration of this article.

had spoken urgently in favour of the promotion of good will between the United States and Great Britain. Gradually, as the Spanish-American War drew on, rumours of an alliance began to appear through the same sources. On May 13, the British ministry, speaking through Joseph Chamberlain, declared themselves in favour of an alliance.[16] In the weeks that immediately followed, the majority of the British press announced themselves in full sympathy with the proposed alliance.

On July 13, the Anglo-American League, representative of the British public, was organized at Stafford House. Its purpose may be stated best in the text of the resolution as it was unanimously adopted. "Considering that the people of the British Empire and the United States are closely allied by blood, inherit the same literature and laws, hold the same principles of self-government, recognize the same ideas of freedom and humanity in the guidance of their National policy and are drawn together by strong common interests in many parts of the world, this meeting is of opinion that every effort should be made in the interests of civilization and of peace to secure the most cordial and constant coöperation on the part of the two nations." [17] The General Committee, which was composed of several hundred individuals, included prominent men from the Government, the church, the universities and colleges, literature, law, manufactur-

[16] Chamberlain, Joseph, "Speech delivered at Birmingham, May 13, 1898," *London Times,* May 14, 1898.

[17] *An American Response to Expressions of English Sympathy* (New York, 1899), introduction.

ing and commerce, banking, and private life.[18]   The honourary officers of the Committee were James Bryce as chairman, the Duke of Sutherland as treasurer, and T. Lee Robert, R. C. Maxwell, and Sir Frederick Pollock as secretaries.

The League met with a very favourable reception in the United States.   Various efforts were made to secure a satisfactory response, and on July 27, the Anglo-American Committee in New York was formed. Its officers included Whitelaw Reid as chairman.   Three members of the committee, Daniel S. Lamont, John G. Carlisle and William C. Whitney, had served in Mr. Cleveland's cabinet.   Three other members, Carl Schurz, Thomas L. James and Benjamin F. Tracy, had served in Republican cabinets.   Two members, John L. Cadwalader and George L. Rives, had served in the department of state.   It included representatives of every administration from Lincoln to McKinley.   It likewise crossed lines both of race and religion, for it included the Frenchman, Frederic R. Coudert; the German, Carl Schurz; the chief Catholic prelate of New York, Archbishop M. A. Corrigan, and the chief Episcopal dignitary, Bishop Henry C. Potter.

The following address was drawn up: "We, citizens of the United States of America, desire to express our most hearty appreciation of the recent demonstrations of sympathy and fellowship with this country on the part of citizens of the various countries comprised in the British Empire.   We earnestly reciprocate these

[18] See *Century Magazine, "A Step toward Universal Peace,"* Vol. LVI (September, 1898), pp. 794-799, for a complete list of the committee.

sentiments, recognizing as we do that the same language and the same principles of ordered liberty should form the basis of an intimate and enduring friendship between these kindred peoples—a friendship destined to hasten the day of peace and good-will among all the nations of the earth."

The address was sent confidentially to about fifteen hundred prominent Americans of every state in the Union representatives of all lines of thought and occupation, who were asked to sign the address if it met with their approval. "Practically none" refused their endorsement. The list of men who thus announced their interest in an Anglo-American friendship was particularly significant in that it included many well-known lawyers and judges, the editors of most of the leading magazines and newspapers, the presidents of most of the standard colleges and universities, leading clergymen of all denominations, representatives of prominent publishing houses, and leaders in finances, business and industry.[19]

After the formation of the two branches of the Anglo-American League, came the next movement for the proposed alliance in the form of an extended magazine publicity. In June, the *Century* in a strong editorial discussed the recent services rendered by Great Britain to the United States. It was a sympathy which was shown in the warmth of the greeting given to Mr. Hay by the members of the royal family at a moment of great tension; in the ill-restrained outburst of cordiality toward us in Parliament; in the well-

[19] See *An American Response to Expressions of English Sympathy* for a complete list of signatures.

timed call of the British Ambasador upon the Captain of the *Maine;* in Sir Julian's discreetly worded address to the President on behalf of the powers; and in the friendly tone of the prominent newspapers in London. "This new interchange of sympathy realizes the statesman's noble vision of race patriotism, and signifies the extinction in America of the anti-British jingo." [20]

During the month of July a number of magazines seemed to indicate that a decided change was taking place in the attitude of both the Americans and the British toward an Anglo-American alliance or understanding. Sentimental arguments, based largely on the theory of a common race, and arguments of mutual trade advantage were lost sight of before the imperative questions of national policy created by the victory of Commodore Dewey in Manila Bay. This was particularly true of the United States for Great Britain, ever since the beginning of the Salisbury ministry, had been largely motivated in her attitude toward the United States by the exigency of her relations with the great European Powers. In general, the discussions of the month considered one of two questions: the conflict between republicanism and monarchy or the protection of British and American interests in the Far East. A few citations will illustrate this conclusion.

"The day," [the Fourth] said the *Century,* "will be distinguished by the omission of the occasional tirades against England. There is no progress of the world that is not marked by somebody's change of mind, and

[20] "A Service of England to America," an editorial, *Century Magazine,* Vol. LVI (June, 1898), p. 314.

in the last three months even the most violent prejudices among our people against our English kinsmen
have disappeared in the face of unmistakable evidence
of her sympathy with America in the irrepressible
conflict between the ideas of the sixteenth century
and those of the nineteenth . . . the two great' di-
visions of the Anglo-Saxon race are "in closer sympathy than ever before." [21]

The *Atlantic Monthly* indicated this change in attitude toward an Anglo-American agreement, in two
significant articles. The first, by James K. Hosmer,
was entitled the "American Evolution. Dependence,
Independence, and Interdependence." "There is no
other kinship among peoples," said Mr. Hosmer, "so
marked as that between the two great branches of the
English-speaking race": the United States, a democracy, and England, both "practically a democratic republic" herself, and "the parent of vast republics."
Only a "moral union" is possible or desirable between
them, but, "The welfare of the world depends upon
their accord; and no other circumstance at the present
moment is so fraught with hope as that, in the midst
of the heavy embarrassments that beset both England
and America, the long-sundered kindred slowly gravi-
tate toward alliance." [22] In the second article, Lord
Bryce first developed Great Britain's foreign relations
and found her isolated and looked upon with jealousy,
if not unfriendliness, by Germany, France, and Russia.

[21] "Reflections Appropriate to 'the Fourth,'" an editorial, *Century
Magazine*, Vol. LVI (July, 1898), p. 474.

[22] Hosmer, James K., "The American Evolution. Dependence, Independence, Interdependence," *Atlantic Monthly*, Vol. LXXXII
(July, 1898), pp. 29-36.

The United States, however, with whom she had ties
of sentiment, of common theories of politics, and of
"common material benefit" held for her "the most
natural affinity and the least likelihood of any clash
of interests." Furthermore, Great Britain would regard the entrance of the United States into the Philippines "with nothing but satisfaction." There were
some obvious difficulties, however, in the way of immediate formal alliance. Meantime, there were certain things which might be done to perpetuate the
good relations which happily prevailed. One was the
conclusion of a general treaty of arbitration, the second was "the agreement to render good services to each
other" such as "giving to a citizen of either nation the
right to invoke the good offices of the diplomatic or
consular representatives of the other in a place where
his own government has no representative"; and the
"recognition of a common citizenship," and, finally,
the realization "that the best and surest foundations
of the future policy of each is to be found in relations
of frank and cordial friendship with the other." [23]

In the same month Frederick Greenwood carried the
new interpretation of an Anglo-American understanding to its logical conclusion. The need for an alliance
on the American side first came with the threat of
European intervention in the Spanish-American War.
On the British side it arose about the time and for
the reason that Mr. Chamberlain spoke of the British
need of alliances. "That it rose on either side at the
prompting of self-interest takes nothing from its

[23] Bryce, James, "The Essential Unity of Britain and America,"
Atlantic Monthly, Vol. LXXXII (July, 1898), pp. 22-29.

worth. If at bottom it really meant partnership in armed defence, it could find base in no other origin to be sound. Say that it sprang from the consideration that 'blood is thicker than water,' and if you really think that you give expression to a stronger or a trustier motive than mutual need you may depend upon it that you are mistaken." Meanwhile, with the victory of Commodore Dewey at Manila and the enthusiastic vote of the House of Representatives, 209 to 91, in favour of the annexation of Hawaii, the United States passed from a national to a world power. Thus another great fighting power had appeared in the world and, as matters stood, that should be to the advantage of Great Britain. According, then, to Mr. Greenwood's theory the alliance had passed from its first stage—one actually of national interest, though it was often concealed under the guise of race sentiment—to its second phase, that of a fighting, imperialistic alliance. The new field of Anglo-American interests was the Far East. [24]

By the middle of July, 1898, it was apparent that the Spanish-American War was practically at an end. Spain had paid her debt of honour to the full and further humiliation was useless. On July 22, the Spanish Government drafted a formal message in behalf of

[24] Greenwood, Frederick, "The Anglo-American Future," *The Nineteenth Century*, Vol. XLIV (July, 1898), pp. 1-11. For further illustrations see *Collier's Weekly*, July 2, 9, 1898; Diplomaticus, "Is there an Anglo-American Understanding," *Fortnightly Review*, Vol. LXX (July, 1898), pp. 163-174; Lecky, W. E. H., "The Relation Between the United States and Other Powers," *Independent*, Vol. L, second half (July, 1898), pp. 15-17; Norman, Henry, "America Revisited in War Time," *McClure's Magazine*, Vol. XI (July, 1898), pp. 297-302.

peace. It was presented four days later to Mr. Mc-
Kinley by Mr. J. Cambon, the French Ambassador.[25]
On July 30, President McKinley submitted the following terms on which peace might be negotiated: first
the relinquishment by Spain of sovereignty over Cuba
and the immediate evacuation of the island; second,
the cession of the island of Porto Rico and one of the
Ladrone islands in lieu of any indemnity; third, the
American occupation of the city, bay and harbour of
Manila "pending the conclusion of a treaty of peace
which shall determine the control, disposition, and government of the Philippines." [26]

On August 7, Spain replied to the terms of peace
offered by the United States. She accepted the first
two, but maintained that the third, relative to the
Philippines, was "quite indefinite." The United States,
said the minister of Spain, cannot believe herself entitled to occupy the bay, the harbour, and the city of
Manila, pending the conclusion of peace, on the ground
of conquest. The Spanish flag still waves over the
city of Manila and the whole archipelago is in the
power and under the sovereignty of Spain.[27]   President McKinley was annoyed at the message and submitted the American terms once more on August 10,
in the form of a formal protocol.[28]   The wording concerning the disposition of the Philippines was exactly
the same as in the previous message. October 1 was
designated as the date for the meeting of the peace

[25] *Foreign Relations*, 1898, pp. 819-820.
[26] *Ibid.*, pp. 820-821.
[27] *Ibid.*, pp. 822-823.
[28] *Ibid.*, pp. 824-825.

commissioners. Two days later the protocol was signed by Secretary Day for the United States and Jules Cambon for Spain.[29] The following day, August 13, General Merritt, aided by Admiral Dewey, completed the capture of Manila.

Thus far during the year, or until the close of the Spanish-American War early in August, Anglo-American friendship had found expression chiefly in three ways: British support for the United States in the prosecution of the war, American coöperation in the British "open door" policy in China, and an attempt to form a general Anglo-American agreement or understanding. Commodore Dewey's victory at Manila had opened the Philippines to exploitation. Should the United States enter upon an imperialistic program and keep possession of the islands, the similarity of her interests and those of Great Britain might lead to a policy of Anglo-American coöperation in the Far East. This would restore to Great Britain her former assurance of a balance of power in European politics. Opportunity for a reciprocal expression of coöperation existed in the West. With the fall of Spanish power in the West Indies, the United States became a close rival of Great Britain for the naval supremacy of the Caribbean Sea. As it was, Great Britain could maintain her prestige there only by stationing a powerful fleet in the Western Atlantic and by holding joint control over any isthmian canal that might be constructed. Such a policy was inexpedient for a number of reasons. It would either necessitate a decided increase in the British naval appropriations or it would weaken the

[29] *Ibid.,* pp. 828-830.

British fleet in the Far East. Besides this, it was almost
sure to incur the ill will of the American people in that
during the last few years they had been steadily developing the theory that they must possess exclusive
control over any isthmian canal. Could the friendship
which was begun between the two peoples during the
Venezuelan boundary controversy, and which had been
steadily developed throughout the two years following,
be maintained and further established, it must naturally lead to a policy of division of power. Whatever
was accomplished, however, would rest not upon governmental negotiations but upon the growing friendship of the people of the two Powers. The United
States would coöperate with Great Britain in order to
establish British supremacy in the Far East. This
would, of course, demand the assurance of the protection of American trade and territorial possessions in
that region. Great Britain would, in turn, yield the
supremacy of the Caribbean together with the control
of the isthmian canal to the United States. In this
case, the American people would guarantee the safety
of the British trade interests and possessions south of
the United States. A consideration of events during
the next few months following the close of the Spanish-American War will show that Anglo-American diplomacy actually developed these two new policies.

As early as the latter part of April, 1898, the British
press began to suggest the results that would attend
the American capture of the Philippines. "If . . . the
United States annexes the Philippines," said the
Statist, and "establishes there not only a coaling station but a strongly fortified port, and if especially it

takes Hawaii as a kind of stepping stone, the change in international relations will be very marked, not merely in the Far East alone, but in Europe as well." Furthermore, if the United States adopts an active policy in China, she will be compelled to take a new attitude in Europe.[30]

Immediately after the battle of Manila, the British press began to consider the disposition of the islands. Certain Americans, it said, wanted to keep them, others wanted to dispose of them—preferably to Great Britain.[31] In the latter case some felt that the maintenance of a coaling station would be sufficient to protect American trade interests.[32] Should the United States annex both Hawaii and the Philippines and a close Anglo-American alliance be formed it would enable the two English speaking peoples to "keep China open to the trade of the world," to prevent "the military Powers from pursuing the policy of grab," and to "render it possible for China to be re-awakened and start once more upon the path of progress."[33] During these same days the American press seldom advocated annexation and seemed to ignore the possibility or necessity of an Anglo-American alliance in the Far East.[34]

About the middle of the month the British press began to recognize a change in the American attitude

[30] *Statist,* April 30, 1898. *Cf. ibid.,* May 7, 1898.

[31] *British Weekly,* May 5, 6, 1898; *Economist,* May 7, 1898; *London Times,* May 4, 1898.

[32] *London Times,* May 4, 1898.

[33] *Statist,* May 7, 1898. *Cf. Pall Mall Gazette,* May 2, 1898; *Chronicle,* May 7, 14, 1898; *Economist,* May 28, 1898.

[34] *Public Opinion,* May 12, 1898; *Chicago Chronicle,* May 14, 1898.

toward the Philippines.[35]   This was expressed first in
the determination of certain Americans to defy European interference in the disposition of the islands. The
United States might trade them to Great Britain for
certain British possessions in the West Indies,[36] or she
might sell them outright.[37]   A few days later it was
suggested that Great Britain looked upon the expansion of American industry with alarm but not hostility.
This was particularly true of the iron industry.[38]   During the last days of the month the press outlined
the future American policy in the islands with a fair
degree of accuracy. The United States would retain
them, herself,[39] setting up some form of a protectorate.
Furthermore, the American policy in the Far East
would be very agreeable to Great Britain. The United
States would demand peace, order, and freedom to
trade everywhere at will subject only to custom house
duties enforced against all nations alike.[40]

British press opinion toward the Philippines was
expressed freely during June. The fact that an agreement had been signed between Great Britain and the
United States whereby the Canadian boundary dispute was referred to a joint high commission seemed to

[35] *Statist,* May 14, 1898.
[36] *Pall Mall Gazette,* May 16, 1898.
[37] *Chronicle,* May 14, 1898.
[38] *Statist,* May 20, 1898.
[39] *British Weekly,* May 28, 1898; *Statist,* May 28, 1898. This report was based upon the departure of American troops for Manila.
[40] *British Weekly,* June 2, 1898; *Economist,* May 28, 1898. This
article also called attention to the idea expressed several weeks later
in the reliable magazines—that the two countries would be "almost
forced into partnership" and though a "business partnership is not
exactly an alliance the distance between them is not very wide."

urge the press to considerable cordiality.[41] As a result the press was quick to note anything that indicated German-American discord.[42]

On June 14, Mr. W. J. Bryan, speaking at Omaha, denounced territorial aggrandizement and advocated giving up the Philippines. About the same time it became equally evident that the Republican party leaders were going to advocate annexation.[43]

Events in China, meanwhile, began to grow serious again. On June 9, 1898, Great Britain leased the island of Lan-tao to the west of Hongkong for 99 years. The Coalition government was not anxious to acquire Chinese territory, but if it could not obtain the establishment of the "open door" it was necessary that British trade interests be protected from the territorial encroachments of the other Powers.[44] The next month, July, 1898, the British flag was raised over Weihai Wei. Fortunately, however, for the safety of Anglo-American trade interests in the East, the United States entered upon a policy of imperialism at the same time that the British supremacy in China was being questioned.

On July 7, President McKinley signed the joint reso-

[41] *British Weekly,* June 2, 1898; *London Times,* June 21, 1898.

[42] *Pall Mall Gazette,* June 6, 10, 11, 15, 1898; *Economist,* June 18, 1898. On June 15, the *Pall Mall Gazette* printed a symposium of American press opinion to show that the United States resented German interference in the Philippines and was disposed to keep the islands herself. On June 21, the same paper said, "Let Germany say that the United States shall not annex the Philippines and there will be an uprising in favor of it."

[43] See *New York Times,* June 21, 22, 1898; *New York Journal,* June 24, 1898; *Pall Mall Gazette,* June 23, 1898.

[44] *Pall Mall Gazette,* June 10, 1898; *British Weekly,* June 10, 1898.

lution which provided for the annexation of the Hawaiian islands. During the previous year, June, 1897, the President had negotiated a treaty which provided for the annexation of the islands. After nine months of fruitless debate the friends of the treaty gave up all hope of being able to secure its ratification. After the victory at Manila sentiment in favour of annexation developed very rapidly. The reasons advanced were almost entirely in behalf of national defense and trade. Hawaii provided a coaling station and a basis of attack only two thousand miles away from San Francisco. Shut out from there an enemy would be thrown back for supplies of fuel to a distance of nearly four thousand miles. But more important than this was the fact that the American commercial interests in the Pacific were too great to be sacrificed. Hawaii was sure to be taken over soon by some nation. If the United States refused to annex it herself, she could not object if another nation took possession of it. Finally, our traditional policy of government was not opposed to annexation.[45] On June 5, a joint resolution in favour of annexation pased the House; on July 6, it was passed by the Senate.

The British looked upon the American acquisition of the islands with hearty favour. This, they said, would silence those Americans who had claimed that Great Britain desired the islands herself and would oppose their annexation by the United States. But, more

[45] *Congressional Record,* 55th Congress, 2d session, Vol. XXXI. pp. 2837, 2866, 2872; *New York Times,* April 30, May 21, June 11, 25, 1898; *London Times,* August 11, 1898; *Chicago Tribune,* June 25, 1898.

significant by far was the fact that Hawaii was but a stepping stone to the Philippines and the Far East. Once in possession of the Hawaiian islands the United States was bound to keep the Philippines. This, in turn would lead the United States to assume an active share in the struggle to maintain the "open door" in China.[46]

After the annexation of Hawaii had been completed the British followed the American attitude toward the Philippines with keen interest. Some said that President McKinley preferred to keep only a coaling station.[47] Others believed that Spain would be left in possession of the islands.[48] Still others were convinced that the United States would keep all of them.[49] They were generally agreed, however, that the United States would tolerate no interference in the ultimate disposition of the islands.[50] None of the European powers, however, would look upon the Americans in the Philippines with favour except the British and the Japanese.[51]

When the American peace commissioners sailed for Paris they left without definite instructions concerning the Philippines. This was probably due to President McKinley's reluctance to act without the full support of the people, and the Americans were not yet prepared to see the full importance of the Philippines in their

[46] *London Times,* March 22, May 6, July 8, 1898; *Economist,* July 9, 1898; *Statist,* July 28, 1898; *New York Tribune,* July 29, 1898.

[47] *Pall Mall Gazette,* July 16, 1898.

[48] *Ibid.,* July 27, 1898.

[49] *Statist,* July 28, 1898; *London Times,* July 30, 1898.

[50] *Statist,* July 9, 28, 1898; *Pall Mall Gazette,* July 5, 1898.

[51] *London Times,* July 29, 1898; *Pall Mall Gazette,* July 28, 1898. *Cf. New York Tribune,* July 28, 1898.

relation to American trade in the East. The letter of
instructions, of September 16, indicated the general
lines of argument used by the imperialists. The American victory in the war had placed upon the nation
certain new duties and responsibilities which "we must
meet and discharge as becomes a great nation on whose
growth and career from the beginning the Ruler of
Nations has plainly written the high command and
pledge of civilization. Incidental to our tenure in the
Philippines is the commercial opportunity to which
American statesmanship cannot be indifferent. It is
just to use every legitimate means for the enlarge-
ment of American trade; but we seek no advantages in
the Orient which are not common to all. Asking only
the open door for ourselves, we are ready to accord
the open door to others." The commercial opportunity
which is associated with this new venture depends
less upon large territorial possessions than "upon an
adequate commercial basis and upon broad and equal
privileges" but the "United States cannot accept less
than the cession in full right and sovereignty of the
island of Luzon." [52]

British sentiment, however, seemed to be assured
that, while the situation in China was becoming more
serious, American sentiment was growing rapidly in
favour of an Anglo-American commercial agreement,[53]

[52] *Foreign Relations,* 1898, pp. 907-908.

[53] See *Pall Mall Gazette,* September 6, 9, 10, 15, 16, 19, 1898;
London Times, September 4, 22, 1898; *British Weekly,* September 25,
1898. By September 16, with the exception of the *Post* and the
World, every important New York paper was advocating the acquisition of the Philippines and the prosecution of a policy of commercial
expansion in the Far East.

under the British policy of the "open door." [54]   On September 13, the *Statist* spoke very specifically. The Continental papers are indulging in their usual quips at Great Britain's expense to the effect that an European alliance against her is imminent and that once the Spanish-American trouble is settled the United States will have little inclination for an Anglo-American alliance. "But in reality our position in China was never so strong as it is at present, *for* not only are we ourselves interested in preventing Russia, Germany, and France—whether singly or in combination—from closing a large part of China against the rest of the world, but so also are the United States and Japan. . . . And what the United States and the British do, Japan will back up. . . . We shall neither allow ourselves to be bullied nor drawn into action that our interests do not require." [55]

One of the strongest assurances of the development of Anglo-American good will was found in the attitude of Germany toward both Great Britain and the United States. By the middle of September Germany was actively attempting to win the friendship of both powers.[56]

During October President McKinley was scheduled to speak at the Trans-Mississippi Exposition at Omaha, Nebraska. He utilized the trip, both going there and returning, to put the Philippine situation

[54] *Cf. Pall Mall Gazette*, September 15, 16, 1898.

[55] See also Temple, Sir Richard, "An Anglo-American versus an European Combination," *North American Review,* Vol. CLXVII, pp. 306-316.

[56] *Statist*, September 10, 1898; *New York Herald*, September 7, 17, 1898.

before the American people. He made no less than sixteen speeches, exclusive of his address at Omaha, to large popular audiences. His theme was always the same. The United States was exceedingly prosperous, her need for a new market was imperative both for the manufacturer and for the farmer, her debt to humanity and civilization opened up to her by her new territorial acquisition must be paid.[57] The reception extended to him both by the people and the press was sufficiently enthusiastic to assure him that the policy of imperialism was growing rapidly in public favour. It was this conclusion that determined his instructions of November 13 to the peace commission.

The peace commission met in Paris, October 1. The American delegation included William R. Day as Chairman, Cushman K. Davis of Minnesota, Chairman of the Senate Committee on Foreign Relations; Senator William P. Frye of Maine, Senator George Gray of Delaware, and Whitelaw Reid, editor of the *New York Tribune* and former ambassador to Germany. The entire month of October was consumed in the discussion of Cuba. On October 31, after the American people had had ample opportunity to express themselves, the real struggle for American expansion began. On November 11, the commissioners asked for definite instructions concerning the Philippines, and on November 13, they were authorized to offer

[57] It is almost impossible to give any definite estimate of the actual influence of these addresses. Mr. McKinley probably spoke to no less than 20,000 or 25,000 people daily for ten days. Complete reports of each of the speeches appeared in most of the papers throughout the country.

Spain between ten and twenty million dollars in payment for the island.[58] Spain accepted the latter amount, under protest, and on December 10, 1898, the treaty was finally signed.[59]

There was little change in Anglo-American relations during the last two months of the year. The British press continued to express satisfaction over the American occupation of the Philippines.[60] On November 4, the New York correspondent of the *Pall Mall Gazette* said, "If Russia closes the treaty port of Newchwang and thus directly raises the 'open door' question, England's subsequent action would appeal powerfully to the sympathy and moral support of the United States." It is recognized that American interests are as great as British in maintaining treaty rights in China.

A number of times during those weeks American audiences paid tribute to Great Britain. One illustration will show the trend of both the British and American feeling. On November 11, General Nelson A. Miles, speaking at a banquet given in his honour in New York, said, "The war has given us reason and opportunity to appreciate our obligations to the mother country." Captain Paget responded, "We shall be proud in the future whenever we see the Stars and Stripes on a warship or a merchantman,

[58] *Foreign Relations*, 1898, p. 945.

[59] *Foreign Relations*, 1898, pp. 831-840; see Cortissoz, Royal, *The Life of Whitelaw Reid* (New York, 1921), Vol. II, pp. 228-235, for Mr. Reid's story of the peace conference.

[60] *London Times*, November 4, 5, 7, 11, 1898; Denby, Sir Charles, "Shall We Keep the Philippines," *Forum*, Vol. XXVI (November, 1898), pp. 278-281; Smalley, *Anglo-American Memories*, pp. 191-194.

for we shall know that on board we have, if not a brother, an ally." [61]

On January 4, 1899, President McKinley transmitted the treaty to the Senate for ratification. It was finally ratified on February 7, after nearly five weeks of bitter debate. During these days of suspense the British press seemed strangely silent. In general, it seemed sure of three facts: that the United States would keep the Philippines; that she would be a successful colonizing nation; and that high colonial tariff duties were not inconsistent with the "open door" policy. On January 6, the *London Times* spoke positively. "A long debate is expected" but "the treaty will be ratified without amendment." On January 12, it said that the treaty would be ratified in spite of the opposition. On January 19, it quoted Senator Davis and Senator Lodge as being sure that the treaty would pass. The following day it accused those senators who were in favour of the Nicaragua canal bill of deliberately trying to postpone debate on the peace treaty until the canal bill was passed. On January 27, it said again that the prospect of ratification without amendment was good. On February 6, it admitted that the fate of the treaty depended on doubtful senators. It still maintained, however, that should the treaty fail on this vote, it would be passed by the next Congress. On February 7, it declared the action of the Senate worthy of congratulation. The *Pall Mall*

[61] *New York Times,* November 12, 1898; *Pall Mall Gazette,* November 12, 1898. For further illustrations, see *London Times,* November 17, 1898; *New York Times,* November 17, 1898, for an account of the annual dinner of the New York Chamber of Commerce, November 16, 1898.

Gazette was equally sure of the action of the Senate. As America must stay in Cuba, it said, so must she stay in the Philippines; foreign intervention is sure.[62]

A typical statement of the British opinion of the ability of the United States as a colonizing nation was given by the *Quarterly Review.* "We have no doubt whatever of the capacity of our kinsmen to grapple effectively with all the difficulties and dangers which they may encounter in the Philippines. We believe that they share the British secret of governing inferior races at a distance with justice and firmness, and with the smallest possible exercise of military power.[63] The *London Times* said the same thing in a briefer way. "Anglo-Saxon vigor will call our latent colonial abilities in the United States." [64]

The third subject of British interest was of peculiar significance. With the possession of the Philippines, the United States became a power in the Far East. Certain Americans had expressed an active sympathy for the British "open door" policy. The question then became this: Would the United States, a high tariff nation, support the "open door" in her new possessions? A high tariff and the "open door" seemed incompatible to many. Furthermore, if the United States did not maintain the "open door" in Hawaii and the Philippines, would she support the British pol-

[62] *Pall Mall Gazette,* January 12, 1898. See also *Statist,* January 7, 1899; Schurz, Carl, "The Issue of Imperialism," Chicago University Convocation Address, January 4, 1899, *Speeches, Correspondence and Political Papers,* Vol. VI, p. 19.

[63] "Democracy and Foreign Affairs," *Quarterly Review,* Vol. CLXXXIX (January, 1899), pp. 241-265.

[64] *London Times,* December 12, 1898. *Cf. Statist,* January 7, 1899.

icy in China? Apparently the British traders soon realized the expediency of finding a way of harmonizing the American tariff and the British "open door." On November 28, 1898, the *Times* suggested that there was no relation between tariff and the "open door." The "open door" meant equality of trade. A few days later the *Statist* assumed the same theory. "High duties are not inconsistent with the 'open door.' What the open door means is that traders of all nationalities shall have equal opportunities, not that there shall be absolute freedom of trade." We have no shadow of doubt that the United States will maintain the open door in the Philippines.[65] There had been one paramount issue for which the British had contended throughout the negotiations concerning the Philippines—the United States must be induced to hold the islands and thereby become a power in the East.[66]

While negotiations had been in progress, Anglo-American friendship had been steadily developing, both in the Caribbean region and in the Pacific. Their first joint action came in the settlement of the Samoan question. The trouble had begun at Apia, April, 1898, when an unfortunate engagement occurred in which one British and two American officers were killed. German treachery was suspected.[67]   Within a few

[65] *Cf. Statist*, December 3, 24, 1898.

[66] *Cf.* Denby, Charles, "Shall We Keep the Philippines," *Forum*, Vol. XXVI (November, 1898), pp. 279-281; Schurz, Carl, Letter to Charles Francis Adams, *Speeches, Letters and Political Papers*, Vol. IV, p. 38; *Hansard's Parliamentary Debates*, Vol. LXVII, p. 503.

[67] *Chronicle*, April 15, 1899; *Independent*, February 23, 1899, suggested that the German policy in Samoa was similar to that of Admiral Diedrichs at Manila. The Germans proposed to join with

days Great Britain agreed to accept the German proposal for the appointment of a joint commission to inquire into the difficulty. Negotiations dragged on for several months. Fortunately, none of the European powers saw fit to intervene. Feeling in Germany continued to grow more bitter.[68] The United States and Great Britain continued to place the responsibility for the loss of lives on the German consul.[69] On November 14, 1899, an agreement was concluded between Germany and Great Britain, subject to the approval of the United States. The United States was to hold Tutuila with its harbour of Pagopago which was really the key to the entire group.[70] Germany received the remainder of the islands. Great Britain was compensated for her loss in the islands in a number of ways. In the first place, she received a number of small islands long desired by the Australian colonies.[71] A demarcation line was drawn between German and British possessions in Africa, and Germany renounced all extraterritorial rights in Zanzibar. Both Germany and the United States agreed that commerce was to be open on equal terms to each of the three nations in all of the islands.[72] The treaty was signed, finally, on December 2, 1899. The United States and Great

the native forces to secure definite possession of the territory. Cf. *Pall Mall Gazette,* March 23, 1899; *Lokal Anzeiger,* March 23, 1899.

[68] *Pall Mall Gazette,* April 14, 1899.

[69] *London Times,* April 14, 1899; *New York Times,* April 13, 1899.

[70] *London Board of Trade Journal,* Vol. XXVII (December, 1899), pp. 737-738.

[71] *Statist,* November 11, 1899; *St. James Budget,* November 17, 1899.

[72] Moore, *International Law Digest,* Vol. I, p. 553.

Britain had acted throughout the entire negotiations in full harmony.[73] Furthermore, in relinquishing all territory in the islands, Great Britain accepted the American possession of Tutuila as a guarantee of British interests in the islands.[74]

While the Anglo-German negotiations were at their height concerning Samoa, the British began their war with the Boers. The test of American friendship was severe for the sympathy of the Americans had always gone instinctively to a people who were struggling for self-government. Nevertheless, throughout the entire war, the United States maintained an attitude of benevolent neutrality highly pleasing and favourable to the British. A few illustrations are significant. The Canadians were allowed to compress a shipment of hay in New York and Boston, consigned for the use of the British forces in South Africa.[75] The hospital ship, *Maine,* was wholly equipped by means of American subscriptions and with an American staff, for service in the Transvaal.[76] The British press considered the President, the Cabinet and the American pub-

[73] *Pall Mall Gazette,* April 25, 1899, quoted Chief Justice Fort of the New Jersey Court of Common Pleas as saying: "The power of unity of purpose of the two nations [Great Britain and the United States] cannot be over-estimated. The Samoan incident proves that if Germany had fired alone, or America or Great Britain had fired alone, international complications beyond estimation might have followed. When England and the United States fired together, there was silence in all the capitals of the world."

[74] *St. James Budget,* November 17, 1899; *Statist,* November 11, 1899; *London Board of Trade Journal,* Vol. XXVII (December, 1899), pp. 737-738; *Pall Mall Gazette,* June 3, 1899.

[75] *Pall Mall Gazette,* November 4, 1899.

[76] *Annual Register,* 1899, part 1, new series, p. 390; *Pall Mall Gazette,* November 7, 1899.

lic friendly toward Great Britain.[77] The reasons usually ascribed by the British for the American friendship were largely those of self-interest rather than sentiment. They had not forgotten British friendship during the Spanish-American War;[78] British coöperation was still necessary in the Philippines;[79] American trade interests desired a British victory;[80] and the United States were engaged in a similar war in the Philippines.[81]

While Great Britain and the United States were becoming more and more closely associated in the East, affairs dragged in the West. The British people generally recognized the necessity for American coöperation in the East, but they were not yet ready to grant reciprocal favours in the West. Soon after the close of actual hostilities in 1898, a few Americans and British began to urge the importance of an isthmian canal to American trade interests in the Far East. Mr. Sidney Low set forth the situation in December, 1898. American trade interests in the Far East and the Pacific are intimately associated with the future of the Isthmus of Panama and the adjacent territories, he said. "The key to the Pacific is the Caribbean sea and the Mexican gulf. Peking and Yokohama may be

[77] *Pall Mall Gazette,* October 9, 1899; quoting from *New York World,* October 9, 1899; *St. James Budget,* May 25, 1900; *Statist,* November 11, 1899; *Chronicle,* April 4, 1900.

[78] *Annual Register,* 1899, part I, new series, p. 390; *Pall Mall Gazette,* February 5, March 2, 21, 1900.

[79] *Pall Mall Gazette,* April 11, 1900.

[80] *St. James Budget,* January 5, 1900; *Chicago Economist,* November 4, 1899.

[81] *Pall Mall Gazette,* May 12; *Chicago Economist,* February 17, 24, 1900.

menaced or defended at Porto Rico, Jamaica, or Santiago de Cuba." The Anglo-American contest for control of the isthmus had at an earlier time culminated in 1850 in the Clayton-Bulwer Treaty. The United States has always been restless under that treaty. America now holds an opening to the East in Hawaii and the Philippines, and a canal has become essential.[82] Two days later, he said, "The United States' trade with the American as well as the Asiatic shores of the Pacific cannot reach its full development so long as the products of industrial districts of the Atlantic seaboard are compelled to take the devious route around Cape Horn." The American Republic is now the dominant power in the Caribbean and the Gulf of Mexico. The only power who could dispute her is England, and her interests are declining. Great Britain refuses to reconsider the Clayton-Bulwer Treaty. Great Britain, in order to hold her control in the Caribbean, would have to station a fleet there as large as at Malta. "And on the other hand the United States can now offer England assistance and support outside the American continent and the American waters, which might, in certain eventualties, prove of the greatest possible value." The abrogation of the Clayton-Bulwer Treaty is quite likely to be suggested by the State Department at no distant date.

The *Bankers' Magazine* saw the need for a canal from a somewhat different point of view. The annexation of Hawaii and the acquisition of the Philippines will render it very necessary that there should be some short route for the navy between the Atlantic and the

[82] *Pall Mall Gazette,* October 5, 1898.

Pacific. The journey of the *Oregon* proved that.[83] During the closing days of the year, Senator George Hoar of Massachusetts, Senator John T. Morgan of Alabama, and Senator Lodge struggled to keep the necessity for the canal before the American people.[84]

The *Economist* suggested another argument. The possibility of war between the United States and Great Britain does not alter the situation since it would be fought in the Atlantic. Paper rights to the canal would not be worth anything. It will always be necessary for the British to maintain a fleet in the West. Meanwhile, it became certain that some definite action was near at hand.

On the same day that the news reached England that the American Senate had ratified the Paris peace treaty, Sir Charles Dilke outlined the new British policy of Anglo-American friendship. "There is a very acute point which concerns our relations with the United States and with regard to that question I think we are in a position to put a definite question to the Government. Some years ago, Great Britain, in conjunction with the Government of France, considered the Clayton-Bulwer Treaty. When the Treaty was last under discussion between the Governments of Great Britain and the United States, Great Britain took up an anti-American attitude, and took up that position in conjunction with the Government of France. The Governments of France and England acted together more or less diplomatically against the Gov-

ernment of the United States. Those of us who have
given much attention to this subject are under the im-
pression that the time has come when the country
ought to make a new departure in this matter; that
we have no interest which ought to lead us to adhere
in this Treaty to the position which in common with
France we took up a good many years ago. If that is
so, . . . we ought to take the first step ourselves by
offering to the United States those conditions as regards the future of the inter-oceanic canal which seem
to us to be good." [85]

Meanwhile, on February 5, 1900, Secretary Hay
and Lord Pauncefote had signed a canal treaty.[86] The
Senate debate on the treaty revealed two weaknesses:
it did not provide for the abrogation of the Clayton-
Bulwer Treaty, and it failed to secure for the United
States the sole right of neutralization and control.
The British *Review of Reviews* stated the attitude of
many of the British toward the objections advanced by
the Senate. The attack by the United States is con-
centrated on the clause by which the United States
binds herself not to fortify the new canal. "This is denounced as a scandalous concession to England, and
all the resources of journalistic vituperation with pen
and pencil have been launched upon the President and
Secretary Hay for their alleged surrender to England.
As a matter of fact, no one in England cares two
straws about the matter and the hubbub on the other
side of the Atlantic has produced no echo here. The
Clayton-Bulwer Treaty has long been an anachron-

---

[85] *Hansard's Parliamentary Debates,* Vol. LXVI, p. 152.
[86] *Senate Documents,* 56th Congress, 1st session, No. 160.

ism, and could not possibly apply to a canal constructed by the United States with its own capital and on its own responsibility." The importance of the outcry against the Nicaraguan Treaty "lies in the evidence which it affords as to the recrudescence of the strong anti-English feeling on the part of the American people." [87] After several months of debate the Senate ratified the amended treaty. The British Government refused to accept the amendments.[88] After the lapse of almost a year a new treaty was submitted, which met the deficiencies of the earlier treaty. It abrogated the Clayton-Bulwer convention and practically placed the canal under the absolute control of the United States.[89] The treaty was finally ratified December 16, 1901. The significance of this act is obvious. British sentiment had developed to the degree which warranted the Government in accepting an unwritten agreement of American protection of British trade in the West in return for American concessions in the Far East.[90]

Throughout the latter part of 1898 it became apparent that Great Britain was not going to be able to maintain her "open door" policy in China. In April, 1899, England and Russia signed an agreement by which England agreed not to seek any railway con-

[87] British *Review of Reviews,* "Isthmian Canal," Vol. XXI (March, 1900), p. 205. *Cf. Statist,* February 10, May 14, December 22, 1900; Rogers, Henry Wade, "The Hay-Pauncefote Treaty," *Forum,* Vol. XXIX (May, 1900), pp. 355-369.

[88] *Moores' International Law Digest,* Vol. III, p. 211.

[89] Latané, John Holladay, *America as a World Power* (New York and London, 1907), p. 207.

[90] *St. James Budget,* October 11, November 22, December 13, 20, 27, 1901.

cessions north of the great wall of China; Russia agreed to give England a free hand south of the wall.[91] American expansion into the East made the maintenance of the British policy essential for her trade interests. Accordingly, on September 6, 1899, Secretary Hay sent notes to the Powers of Europe requesting a declaration of their interests in China.

The note which was sent to Great Britain is typical of the others: "It is the sincere desire of my Government that the interests of its citizens may not be prejudiced through exclusive treatment by any of the controlling Powers within their respective 'spheres of interest' in China, and it hopes to retain there an open market for all the world's commerce, remove dangerous sources of international irritation, and thereby hasten united action of the Powers at Peking to promote administrative reforms so greatly needed for strengthening the Imperial Government and maintaining the integrity of China, in which it believes the whole Western world alike is concerned. It believes that such a result may be greatly aided and advanced by declarations of the various Powers claiming 'spheres of interest' in China as to their intentions in regard to the treatment of foreign trade and commerce therein, and that the present is a very favourable moment for informing Her Majesty's Government of the desire of the United States to have it make on its own part, and to lend its powerful support in the effort to obtain

[91] *Sessional Papers,* 1900, Vol. CV (State Papers, Vol. LIX), Correspondence respecting affairs in China; *Congressional Record,* Vol. XXXIII, part 4 (56th Congress, 1st session), p. 3408. *House Document* No. 547, 56th Congress, 1st session, Vol. XCVIII.

from each of the various Powers claiming 'spheres of interest' in China a declaration substantially to the following effect: (1) That it will in no way interfere with any Treaty port or any vested interest within any so-called 'sphere of interest' or leased territory it may have in China. (2) That the Chinese Treaty Tariff of the time being shall apply to all merchandise landed or shipped to all such ports as are within such 'sphere of interest' no matter to what nationality it may belong, and that duties leviable shall be collected by the Chinese Government. (3) That it will levy no higher harbor duties on vessels of another nationality frequenting any port in such 'sphere' than shall be levied on vessels of its own nationality." [92]

Lord Salisbury submitted his reply on November 30. "I have much pleasure in informing your Excellency that Her Majesty's Government will be prepared to make a declaration in the sense desired by your Government in regard to the leased territory of Wei-hai-Wei and territory in China which may hereafter be acquired by Great Britain by lease or otherwise," provided that similar declarations may be obtained by the other Powers concerned.[93] Favourable returns were received from each of the other powers. France replied on December 16, Russia on December 30, 1899, and Berlin on February 19, 1900. On March 30, 1900, the United States notified the European Powers that the notes had been agreed to by each and that the

---

[92] *Sessional Papers*, Vol. CV (State Papers, Vol. LIX), Correspondence respecting foreign trade in China; *House Document* No. 5475, 56th Congress, 1st session, Vol. XCVIII.

[93] *Ibid.*

policy proposed would be considered effective.[94]   Apparently each of the powers had been afraid to refuse assent to a policy which was supported by both the United States and Great Britain.

Thus the United States, under the leadership of John Hay, had completed the work begun by Great Britain early in 1898. The reason for the success of Mr. Hay seems obvious.   In 1898, Great Britain had stood alone in her demands upon the European powers.   In 1900, the commercial relation of the United States and Great Britain in the Far East was so clearly established that the Continental Powers dare not risk opposition to the American demand for the "open door." [95]   The United States had accomplished what Great Britain tried to do two years earlier.

[94] *Ibid.*

[95] *Brooklyn Daily Eagle,* January 5, 6, March 16, 28, 1900; *New York Times,* January 6, 18, February 19, 1900; *London Times,* January 10, 15, February 20, 1900; *Pall Mall Gazette,* November 23, 1899; *St. James Budget,* March 20 1900; *Economist,* November 11, 1899; *Spectator,* December 9, 1899, April 4, 1900.

BIBLIOGRAPHY

PRIMARY SOURCES

a. *Government Documents*

"Affairs in Cuba," *Report of the Committee on Foreign Relations, United States Senate.* 55th Congress, 2d session, Report No. 885, 1898. The same material was also published by order of the 56th Congress, 2d session, as *Senate Document* No. 231, part 7, 1901. Government Printing Office, Washington, 1898.

The Annual Register, A Review of Public Events at Home and Abroad. New series, 1897-1901. Longmans, Green & Co., London, New York, Bombay.

Annual Report of Navy Department, 1898. The same material was also published by order of the 55th Congress, 3d session, as *House Document*, Vol. XII, No. 3. Government Printing Office, Washington, 1899.

Annual Report of the War Department, 1898. Government Printing Office, Washington, 1899.

British and Foreign State Papers. Vol. LXXXIX (1896-1897), Vol. XCII (1899-1900). Harrison & Sons, London, 1897-1900.

Bryan, L. Henry, compiler, *Compilation of Treaties in Force July 7, 1898.* 55th Congress, 3d session, *House Document*, No. 276. Government Printing Office, Washington, 1899.

Commercial Relations of the United States with Foreign Countries, 1891-1896. Annual volumes. Government Printing Office, Washington.

"Communications in the Office of Naval Operations," *Cipher Messages.* Vol. II.

Congressional Record. 54th Congress, 1st session, Vol. XXVIII, part 1 (December, 1895); 57th Congress, 1st session, Vol. XXXV, part 1 (December, 1901). Government Printing Office, Washington.

"Correspondence Respecting the Affairs of China," *Accounts and Papers*. Vol. LIV (State Papers, Vol. LV). *Parliamentary Papers*. Vol. CV, 1898. London, 1898.

"Correspondence Respecting the Proposals on Currency, made by the Special Envoys from the United States," Enclosure 2 in No. II, *Parliamentary Papers*. Vol. CV, 1898. London, 1898.

Ellis, George D., compiler, *Platforms of the Two Great Political Parties*. Government Printing Office, Washington, 1920.

Grimshaw, W. H., compiler, *Miscellaneous Documents and Speeches on Cuba and Philippines, 1897-1899*. Government Printing Office, Washington, 1899.

Grimshaw, W. H., compiler, *Tariff, International Bank and Miscellaneous Speeches—Trust, Free Silver and War Revenue, 1897-1899*. Government Printing Office, Washington, 1899.

Journal of the Executive Proceedings of the Senate. Vols. XXX-XXXI. Government Printing Office, Washington, 1909.

Moore, John Bassett, ed., *A Digest of International Law*. 8 v. Government Printing Office, Washington, 1906. Also published by order of 56th Congress, 2d session, as *House Document*, No. 556, 1900-1901.

Papers Relating to the Foreign Relations of the United States, 1895-1901. Government Printing Office, Washington.

The Parliamentary Debates (Hansard's). Fourth series, Vol. VL (January 19, 1897); Vol. IXC (August, 1901). Wyman & Sons, London.

Richardson, James D., ed., *A Compilation of the Messages and Papers of the Presidents, 1789-1897*. 10 v. Government Printing Office, Washington, 1898; Supplement, 1897-1902, compiled and arranged by George Raymond Devitt, Bureau of National Literature and Art, Washington, 1903.

The Statutes at Large of the United States of America. Vols. XXVIII, XXIX. Government Printing Office, Washington.

"United States Naval Intelligence," *Information from Abroad.* Numbers 1-8. Government Printing Office, Washington, 1899-1900.

"War Notes," No. 1, Office of Naval Intelligence, *Information from Abroad,* 1898.

b. *Correspondence, Speeches, Memoirs and Autobiographies.*

Allen, Lieutenant W. H., "The Voyage of the Oregon," *The American-Spanish War—A History by the War Leaders.* Chas. C. Haskell and Son, Norwich, Conn., 1899.

An American Response to Expressions of English Sympathy. Printed for the Anglo-American Committee, New York, 1899.

The American-Spanish War—A History by the War Leaders. Chas. C. Haskell and Son, Norwich, Conn., 1899.

Archer, William, *America To-day.* Charles Scribner's Sons, New York, 1899. A series of letters and essays which first appeared in the London *Pall Mall Gazette,* the *Pall Mall Magazine,* and the *New York Times.*

Barrett, John, *Admiral George Dewey. A Sketch of the Man.* Harper & Brothers, New York and London. 1899.

Atkins, John Black, *The War in Cuba, the Experiences of an Englishman with the United States Army.* Smith, Elder & Co., London, 1899.

Beresford, Lord Charles, *The Break-up of China, an Account of its Present Commerce, Currency, Waterways, Armies, Railways, Police and Future Prospects.* Harper & Brothers, New York and London, 1899.

Bryan, William J., *The First Battle.* W. B. Conkey Company, Chicago, 1897.

Calkins, Lieutenant C. G., "The Naval Battle of Manila,"

The American-Spanish War—A History by the War Leaders. Chas. C. Haskell & Son, Norwich, Conn., 1899.

Chamberlain, Joseph, *Mr. Chamberlain's Speeches.* Chas. W. Boyd, ed. 2 v. Constable and Company, London, 1914.

Dewey, George, *Autobiography of George Dewey.* C. Scribner's Sons, New York, 1913.

Dickens, Charles, *American Notes.* The Macmillan Company, London and New York, 1893.

Eckardstein, Baron von, *Ten Years at the Court of St. James, 1895-1905.* Translated and edited by Prof. George Young. Thornton Butterworth, London, 1912.

Evans, Robley D., *A Sailor's Log, Recollections of Forty Years of Naval Life.* Appleton and Company, New York, 1901.

Gladden, Washington, *England and America.* Addresses delivered in England during the summer of 1898. J. Clarke & Co., London, 1898.

Hale, S. Reynolds, *A Little Tour in America.* Edward Arnold, London and New York, 1895.

Harvey, William Hope, *Coin's Financial School.* Coin Publishing Company, Chicago, 1894.

Harvey, William Hope, *A Tale of Two Nations.* Coin Publishing Company, Chicago, 1894.

Hay, John, *Addresses of John Hay.* The Century Company, New York, 1907.

Hoar, George F., *Autobiography of Seventy Years.* C. Scribner's Sons, New York, 1903.

Hobson, Richmond Pearson, *The Sinking of the Merrimac.* The Century Company, New York, 1899.

Hurd, Archibald, *An Incident of War.* Sir Joseph & Sons, London, 1916.

Kipling, Rudyard, *American Notes.* Frank F. Lovell Co., New York, 1899.

McCarthy, Justin, "What England Feels," *The American-Spanish War—A History by the War Leaders.* Chas. C. Haskell & Son, Norwich, Conn., 1899.

Mackay, Alexander, *The Western World,* or *Travels in the*

United States in 1846-1847. Lea & Blanchard, Philadelphia, 1849.

McKinley, William, *Speeches and Addresses of William McKinley.* March 1, 1897–May 30, 1900. Doubleday & McClure Co., New York, 1900.

Palmer, Frederick, *George Dewey, Admiral: Impressions of Dewey and the Olympia on their Homeward Progress from Manila.* Doubleday & McClure Co., New York, 1899.

Reid, Whitelaw, "Our New Duties," *A Commencement Address at the Seventy-fifth Anniversary of Miami University, June 15, 1899.* Printed for the University, New York, 1899.

Roberts, George E., *Coin at School and in Finance.* W. B. Conkey Company, Chicago, 1895.

Schurz, Carl, *Speeches, Correspondence and Political Papers of Carl Schurz.* Frederic Bancroft, ed. 6 v. G. P. Putnam's Sons, New York, 1913.

Smalley, George W., *Anglo-American Memories,* second series. 2 v. Duckworth & Co., London, 1912.

Stickney, Joseph L., *Life and Glorious Deeds of Admiral Dewey.* C. B. Ayer Company, Chicago, 1898.

Thayer, William Roscoe, *Life and Letters of John Hay.* 2 v. Houghton Mifflin Company, Boston and New York, 1915.

Trollope, Frances, *Domestic Manners of the Americans.* 2 v. Dodd, Mead and Company, New York, 1894.

Watson, William, "England to America," *The Purple East.* John Lane Company, London, 1896.

White, Andrew Dickson, *Autobiography,* 2 v. The Century Company, New York, 1905.

White, Trumbull, *Silver and Gold.* Publisher's Union, Chicago, 1895.

c. *Newspapers and Weekly Periodicals*

Chicago, Ill.: *Daily Inter Ocean,* January 1, 1897 to March 15, 1898.

Chicago, Ill.: *The Economist, A Weekly Financial, Com-*

mercial and Real Estate Newspaper, January, 1898, to June, 1900; July to December, 1901.

London, Eng.: *British Weekly,* January, 1897, to March, 1902.

London, Eng.: *The Economist, A Weekly Commercial Times, Bankers' Gazette and Railway Monitor,* January, 1897, to December, 1901.

London, Engl.: *The Graphic,* January to December, 1898.

London, Engl: *Illustrated London News,* 1898.

London, Engl: *London Gazette,* April 26, 1898.

London, Engl.: *The Pall Mall Gazette,* January, 1897, to March, 1902.

London, Engl: *Saturday Review,* 1897 to 1898.

London, Engl: *Spectator,* January, 1897, to March, 1902.

London, Engl.: *The Statist, A Journal of Practical Finance and Trade.* January, 1897, to March, 1902.

London, Engl.: *St. James Budget,* March, 1898, to March, 1902.

London, Engl: *London Times,* January 1, 1897, to March 15, 1902.

Manchester, Engl: *Northern Trade and Finance,* October 1, 1897, to January 1, 1898.

Montreal, Can.: *Montreal Gazette,* January 1, 1898, to July 15, 1898.

New York, N. Y.: *The Bankers' Magazine,* January 1, 1897, to March 15, 1902.

New York, N. Y.: *Bradstreet's,* January to June, 1898.

New York, N. Y.: *The Commercial and Financial Chronicle,* January, 1898, to December, 1900.

New York, N. Y.: *New York Evening Post,* January 1 to 31, 1898.

New York, N. Y.: *New York Herald,* January 1, 1898, to March 1, 1902.

New York, N. Y.: *New York Journal,* April 1, 1898, to September 15, 1898, *passim.*

New York, N. Y.: *Literary Digest,* December, 1895, to March, 1902.

New York, N. Y.: *Public Opinion*, December, 1895, to March, 1902.

New York, N. Y.: *New York Times*, January 1, 1897, to March 15, 1902.

New York, N. Y.: *New York Tribune*, January 1, 1898, to March 1, 1902.

New York, N. Y.: *Wall Street Journal*, June 1, 1900, to December 31, 1901.

New York, N. Y.: *New York World*, April 1, 1898, to September 15, 1898, *passim*.

Ottawa, Can.: *Ottawa Citizen*, January 1, 1898, to July 15, 1898.

Toronto, Can.: *Toronto Globe*, January 1, 1898, to July 15, 1898.

d. *Articles*

Abbott, Lyman, "The Basis of an Anglo-American Understanding," *North American Review*, Vol. CLXVI (May, 1898), pp. 513-521.

Adams, Brooks, "The Spanish War and the Equilibrium of the World," *Forum*, Vol. XXV (August, 1898), pp. 641-651.

"American Greetings and Tributes to Britain," a body of selected verse, *Review of Reviews*, Vol. XXVIII (July, 1898), pp. 71-73.

Archer, William, "America and the English Language," *Pall Mall Magazine*, Vol. XVI (October, 1898), pp. 231-235.

Bryce, James, "The Essential Unity of Britain and America," *Atlantic Monthly*, Vol. LXXXII (July, 1898), pp. 22-29.

[By a Canadian Liberal], "The Anglo-American Joint High Commission," *North American Review*, Vol. CLXVII (August, 1898), pp. 165-175.

Carnegie, Andrew, "Distant Possessions—The Parting of the Ways," *North American Review*, Vol. CLXVII (August, 1898), pp. 239-248.

Chamberlain, Rt. Hon. Joseph, "Recent Developments of a Policy in the United States and their Relation to an Anglo-American Alliance," *Scribner's Magazine*, Vol., XXIV (December, 1898), pp. 674-682.

Clarke, Sir George Sydenham, "England and America," *Nineteenth Century*, Vol. XLIV (August, 1898), pp. 186-195.

Copeland, Walter, "An Anglo-American Alliance," *Westminster Review*, Vol. CL (August, 1898), pp. 168-170.

"The Crisis in America," *Edinburgh Review*, Vol. CLXXXV (April, 1897), pp. 382-404.

Crowninshield, Captain A. S., "Advantages of the Nicaragua Canal," *Century Magazine*, Vol. LVII (January, 1899), pp. 458-466.

Denby, Charles, "Shall We Keep the Philippines?" *Forum*, Vol. XXVI (November, 1898), pp. 279-291.

Dicey, Albert Venn, "England and America," *Atlantic Monthly*, Vol. LXXXII (October, 1898), pp. 441-445.

Dicey, Edward, "The New American Imperialism," *Nineteenth Century*, Vol. XLIV (September, 1898), pp. 487-501.

Dilke, Charles, "An Anglo-American Alliance," *Pall Mall Magazine*, Vol. XVI (September, 1898), pp. 37-38.

Dilke, Charles, "The Future Relations of Great Britain and the United States," *Forum*, Vol. XXVI (January, 1898), pp. 521-528.

Dilke, Sir Charles; Barrett, Hon. John; Lusk, Hugh H., "The Problem of the Philippines," *North American Review*, Vol. CLXXVII (September, 1898), pp. 257-277.

[Diplomaticus], "Is there an Anglo-American Understanding?" *Fortnightly Review*, Vol. LXX (July, 1898), pp. 163-174.

Dunnell, Mark B., "Our Policy in China," *North American Review*, Vol. CLXVII (October, 1898), pp. 393-408.

Fisher, Horace N., "The Development of our Foreign policy," *Atlantic Monthly*, Vol. LXXII (October, 1898), pp. 552-559.

Flower, B. O., "The Proposed Federation of the Anglo-Saxon Nations," *Arena,* Vol. XX (August, 1898), pp. 223-239.

Gladden, Washington, "Are the Americans Anglo-Saxons?" *Spectator,* Vol. LXXX (July 30, 1898), pp. 614-615.

Greenwood, Frederick, "The Anglo-American Future," *Nineteenth Century,* Vol. XLIV (July, 1898), pp. 1-11.

Hobson, Richmond Pearson, "The Sinking of the Merrimac," *Century Magazine,* Vol. LVII (December, 1898), pp. 265-283, (January, 1898), pp. 427-450, (February, 1899), pp. 580-604, (March, 1899), pp. 752-779.

Hosmer, James K., "The American Evolution, Dependence, Independence, Interdependence," *Atlantic Monthly,* Vol. LXXXII (July, 1898), pp. 29-36.

Kelly, Edmund, "An American in Madrid during the War," *Century Magazine,* Vol. LVII (January, 1899), pp. 450-457.

Lecky, W. E. H., "The Relation Between the United States and Other Powers," *Independent,* Vol. L, second half (July, 1898), pp. 15-17.

Loud, Colonel George A.; Kindleberger, Dr. Charles P.; Evans, Joel C., "The Battle of Manila," *Century Magazine,* Vol. LVI (September, 1898), pp. 611-627.

Low, Sidney, "The Change in English Sentiment toward the United States," *Forum,* Vol. XXVI (November, 1898), pp. 364-373.

McDermot, Rev. George, "The Anglo-American Alliance and the Irish-Americans," *Catholic World,* Vol. LXVIII (October, 1898), pp. 75-88.

Mahan, A. T.; "The Future in Relation to American Naval Power," *Harper's New Monthly Magazine,* Vol. XCI (October, 1895), pp. 767-775.

Mahan, A. T., "Hawaii and Our Future Sea Power," *Forum,* Vol. XV (March, 1893), pp. 1-11.

Mahan, A. T., "The Isthmus and Sea Power," *Atlantic Monthly,* Vol. LXII (October, 1893), pp. 459-473.

Mahan, A. T., "Possibilities of Anglo-American Reunion,"

North American Review, Vol. CLIX (November, 1894), pp. 551-573.

Mahan, A. T., "The United States Looking Outward," *Atlantic Monthly,* Vol. LXIV (December, 1890), pp. 816-824.

Matthews, Byron C., "A Study in Nativities," *Forum,* Vol. XXVI (January, 1898), pp. 621-632.

Mills, Hon. David, "Which Shall Dominate—Saxon or Slav?" *North American Review,* Vol. CLXVI (June, 1898), pp. 729-739.

"Money and Masses in America," *Quarterly Review,* Vol. CLXXXIV (October, 1896), pp. 564-588.

Norman, Henry, "America Revisited in War Time," *McClure's Magazine,* Vol. XI (July, 1898), pp. 297-302.

Olney, Richard, "International Isolation of the United States," *Atlantic Monthly,* Vol. LXXXI (May, 1898), pp. 577-588.

O'Shea, John J., "The Irish Leaven in American Progress," *Forum,* Vol. XXVII (May, 1899), pp. 285-296.

Persins, Captain Von L., "How Manila Surrendered," *The Living Age,* Vol. CCCXVIII (September 15, 1923), pp. 500-505.

[Politicus], "The Collision of the Old World and the New," *Contemporary Review,* Vol. LXXIII (May, 1898), pp. 609-617.

Ralph, Julian, "Anglo-Saxon Affinities," *Harper's Magazine,* Vol. XCVIII (February, 1899), pp. 385-391.

Redpath, John Clark, "The United States and the Concert of Nations," *Arena,* Vol. XX (August, 1898), pp. 145-167.

"Reflections Appropriate to the Fourth," *Century Magazine,* Vol. LVI (July, 1898), p. 474.

Reid, Whitelaw, "The Territory with Which We are Threatened," *Century Magazine,* Vol. LVI (September, 1898), pp. 788-794.

Ross, Edward Alsworth, "England as an Ally," *Arena,* Vol. XXIII (June, 1900), pp. 583-592.

Sampson, Rear-Admiral William T., "The Atlantic Fleet

in the Spanish War," *Century Magazine*, Vol. LVII (April, 1899), pp. 886-912.

Schurz, Carl, "The Anglo-American Friendship," *Atlantic Monthly*, Vol. LXXXII (October, 1898), pp. 433-440.

Schurz, Carl, "Thoughts on American Imperialism," *Century Magazine*, LVI (September, 1898), pp. 781-788.

"A Service of England to America," editorial, *Century Magazine*, Vol. LVI (June, 1898), p. 314.

Shriver, Edwin J., "Silver Politics Across Seas," *Westminster Review*, Vol. CXLVI (November, 1896), pp. 487-497.

"The Spanish Crisis," *Blackwood's Magazine*, Vol. CLXIII (February, 1898), pp. 238-253.

"A Step Toward Universal Peace," *Century Magazine*, Vol. LVI (September, 1898), pp. 794-799.

Temple, Richard, "Anglo-American versus European Combination," *North American Review*, Vol. CLXVII (September, 1898), pp. 306-317.

Tourgée, Albion W., "The Twentieth Century Peace-Makers," *Contemporary Review*, Vol. LXXV (June, 1899), pp. 886-908.

"The United States and Spain," *Quarterly Review*, Vol. CLXXX (July, 1898), pp. 216-241.

Vanderlip, Frank A., "Facts About the Philippines," *Century Magazine*, Vol. LVI (August, 1898), pp. 555-563.

Waldstein, Charles, "The English-Speaking Brotherhood," *North American Review*, Vol. CLXVII (August, 1898), pp. 223-238.

Wheeler, Benjamin Ide, "The Old World in the New," *Atlantic Monthly*, Vol. LXXXII (August, 1898), pp. 145-153.

SECONDARY SOURCES

e. Books and Monographs

Adams, George Burton, *Why Americans Dislike England*. Henry Altemus, Philadelphia, 1896.

Alger, R. A., *The Spanish-American War*. Harper & Brothers, New York and London, 1901.

Altschul, Charles, *The American Revolution in our Text-books*. George H. Doran Company, New York, 1917.

Benton, Elton J., *International Law and Diplomacy of the Spanish-American War*. The Johns Hopkins Press, Baltimore, 1908.

Callahan, James Morton, "American Relations in the Pacific and Far East, 1784-1900." *Johns Hopkins University Studies in Historical and Political Science*, series XIX, Nos. 1-3. Johns Hopkins Press, Baltimore, 1901.

Callahan, James Morton, "Cuba and Anglo-American Relations," *Annual Report of the American Historical Association, 1897*, pp. 195-215, Washington, 1898.

Callahan, James Morton, *Cuba and International Relations, A Historical Study in American Diplomacy*. Johns Hopkins Press, Baltimore, 1899.

Chadwick, French Ensor, *The Relations of the United States and Spain, the Spanish-American War*. 2 v. C. Scribner's Sons, New York, 1911.

Cook, J. G., *Anglophobia, an Analysis of anti-British Prejudice in the United States*. The Four Seas Company, Boston, 1919.

Coolidge, Archibald Cary, *The United States as a World Power*. The Macmillan Company, New York, 1912.

Cortissoz, Royal, *The Life of Whitelaw Reid*. 2 v. Charles Scribner's Sons, New York, 1921.

Dawson, Thomas Fulton, *Life and Character of Edward Oliver Wolcott*. 2 v. The Knickerbocker Press, New York, 1911.

Dos Passos, John R., *The Anglo-Saxon Century and the Unification of the English-Speaking People*. Putnam's Sons, New York, 1902.

Dunning, William Archibald, *The British Empire and the United States, a Review of their Relations during the Century of Peace following the Treaty of Ghent*. Charles Scribner's Sons, New York, 1914.

Fish, Carl Russell, *American Diplomacy*. Henry Holt and Company, New York, 1915.

Gardiner, A. G., *The Anglo-American Future*. Thomas Seltzer, New York, 1912.

Gardiner, Charles Alexander, *The Proposed Anglo-American Alliance*, an address delivered before the American Social Science Association at its Annual Meeting at Saratoga, August 31, 1898. G. P. Putnam's Sons, New York, 1898.

Harrison, Mrs. Burton, *The Anglomaniacs*. The Century Company, New York, 1899.

Hart, Albert Bushnell, *The Monroe Doctrine, an Interpretation*. Little, Brown and Company, Boston, 1917.

Hart, Albert Bushnell, Preface to *Documents, 39-49*. Association for International Conciliation, New York, 1911.

Hart, Albert Bushnell, *School Books and International Prejudices*. American Association for International Conciliation, New York, 1911.

Keim, Jeanette, *Forty Years of German-American Political Relations*, University of Pennsylvania Series, 1919.

Kraft, Herman Frederick, and Norris, Walter B., *Sea Power in American History*. The Century Company, New York, 1920.

Latané, John Holladay, *America as a World Power* (Albert Bushnell Hart, ed., *The American Nation: a History*, Vol XXV). Harper & Brothers, New York, 1907.

Latané, John Holladay, *From Isolation to Leadership, a Review of American Foreign Policy*. Doubleday, Page & Company, New York, 1918.

Latané, John Holladay, *The United States and Latin America*. Doubleday, Page & Company, New York, 1920.

Lodge, Henry Cabot, *The War with Spain*. Harper & Brothers, New York and London, 1899.

Long, John D., *The New American Navy*. 2 v. The Outlook Company, New York, 1903.

Low, Sidney, and Sanders, L. C., *History of England During the Reign of Queen Victoria* (William Hunt and R. L. Poole, ed., *The Political History of England*, Vol. XII.) Longmans, Green and Company, London, 1907.

Mahan, Captain A. T., *Lessons of the War with Spain*. Little, Brown and Company, Boston, 1899.

Marburg, Theodore, *The War with Spain*. John Murphy & Company, Baltimore, 1898.

O'Brien, R. B., *Life of Charles Stewart Parnell, 1846-1891*. 2 v. Harper & Brothers, New York, 1898.

Olcott, Charles S., *William McKinley* (*American Statesman*, second series). 2 v. Houghton, Mifflin Company, New York, 1916.

Prince, Morton, *Psychology of the Kaiser*. Richard G. Badger, Boston, 1915.

Reid, Whitelaw, *American and English Studies*. Charles Scribner's Sons, New York, 1913.

Reid, Whitelaw, *Problems of Expansion*. The Century Company, New York, 1900.

Schieber, Clara Eve, *The Transformation of American Sentiment Towards Germany, 1870-1914*. The Cornhill Company, Boston, 1923.

Streator, Martin Lyman, *The Anglo-American Alliance in Prophecy; or, The Promises to the Fathers*. Our Race Publishing Company, New Haven, Conn., 1900.

Taylor, C. Carlisle, *Life of Admiral Mahan*. George H. Doran Company, New York, 1920.

Wister, Owen, *A Straight Deal or the Ancient Grudge*. The Macmillan Company, New York, 1920.

Whates, H., *The Third Salisbury Administration 1895-1900*. Vacher & Sons, Westminster, 1900.

INDEX